THE REAL ME
IS GONNA
BE A SHOCK

JILL SOLNICKI

# THE REAL ME IS GONNA BE A SHOCK

### A YEAR IN THE LIFE
### OF A FRONT-LINE TEACHER

Lester Publishing Limited

Canadian Cataloguing in Publication Data

Solnicki, Jill
The real me is gonna be a shock

ISBN 1-895555-28-0

1. Problem children – Education – Ontario. 2. Juvenile delinquents – Education – Ontario. 3. Literature – Study and teaching (Secondary) – Ontario. 4. Special education – Ontario. 5. Teachers of problem children – Ontario. I. Title.

LC4803.C32056 1992      371.93'09713      C92-093037-9

"My Papa's Waltz", copyright 1942 by Hearst Magazines, Inc. from *The Collected Poems of Theodore Roethke*. Used by permission of Doubleday, a division of Bantam Doubleday Dell Publishing Group, Inc.
*Anne Frank: The Diary of a Young Girl*, copyright 1952 by Otto H. Frank. Used by permission of Doubleday, a division of Bantam Doubleday Dell Publishing Group, Inc.

Text and jacket design: Counterpunch/David Vereschagin

Lester Publishing Limited
56 The Esplanade
Toronto, Ontario
M5E 1A7

Printed and bound in Canada.

92 93 94 95  5 4 3 2 1

# AUTHOR'S NOTE

While the location for *The Real Me Is Gonna Be a Shock* is Toronto, the kind of school described in this book exists in many other places: it is called a vocational school in parts of Canada, a secondary modern in Britain, a *Technische Hochschule* in Germany, and so on.

The special school described in this book is not to be confused with the schools run for the blind, the deaf, etc. The type of school described here had its origins in the two-year vocational schools first established in the 1960s, to provide training in a trade to students who were judged to be unable to handle the academic demands of the regular high schools. As time passed, the special schools evolved. When "streaming" was established in the Ontario secondary school curriculum, dividing the curriculum into the advanced level, which could lead to university, the general level, and the basic level, these schools granted a four-year diploma at the basic level. A more recent change in the evolution of the special school has been to introduce some general-level courses.

For the past ten years I have been a teacher at several special schools. This book is based on journals that I kept over that period of time. The incidents that comprise this book are authentic, based on my experiences. The student characters are composite portraits; the teachers are fictitious characters developed to help represent and dramatize the realities of teaching in a special school.

Some of the student poems and stories found in the book were first published in several magazines issued by a special school. "My Papa's Waltz," by Theodore Roethke, and segments of *The Diary of Anne Frank* are published with the permission of the publisher.

A number of people contributed to this book in different ways. I would like to thank my brother, Dr. Peter Newman, my sister-in-law, Renée Bouthot, and my nieces and nephew, Leorra, Dana, and Adam, for generously providing me with a "room of my own" where I could write; Susan and Howard Roher, for opening their home to me when I continued to be a peripatetic writer; and my sister, Erna Paris, and brother-in-law, Tom Robinson, who bolstered me from the reservoir of their own considerable writing experience.

I would like to thank my editor, Margaret Allen, to whom I first showed the manuscript, for her excellent suggestions and direction; Robin Skelton, who helped to shape the book, and continued the generosity that he has bestowed on all my writing endeavours; Beverley Slopen, my agent, for her enthusiastic assistance; and Malcolm Lester and Kathy Lowinger, of Lester Publishing, who received the book so warmly, and gave me their vote of confidence.

I would also like to thank fellow teachers Jan Snider, Liz Dickens, Myrna Freedman, Heidi Giblon, Dave Taylor and Robin Ayres, for their support; and to express my gratitude to the myriad students, too numerous to mention, who explained their terms, their codes, and their symbols, opening to me the doors of their adolescent world, and their private lives.

I would especially like to acknowledge the role of my immediate family: my daughter and my son, Lara and Daniel, who cheerfully accommodated themselves to the inconveniences of a writing mother; and most of all, my husband, Victor. It was he who suggested that the daily anecdotes I brought home from my teaching could become a book, who encouraged me when I wavered, whose creative suggestions helped me over rocky terrain, and whose talents and editorial skills enhanced this book in untold ways.

Thank you.

Jill Solnicki

For my children, Lara and Daniel,
and for all the other children.

1

■

# BEGINNINGS

Ahead, on a low hill, stood the yellow-brick building that was my destination this morning. Behind me, reflected in my rear-view mirror, were pools of shadow lying on the road. Now I was turning down a driveway, past a flag-pole, into a large parking lot; and now squeezing my car into a space between sensible teacher cars – station wagons, small American coupés, their back seats tumbling with baby paraphernalia, books, sports equipment. I wouldn't park near the fence, in the student area, where the battered cars and beat-up trucks sat.

Staring back at me from the rear-view mirror was a pale face, the eyes tentative. I couldn't put it off any longer. I had to open the car door. I had to make my move.

Scruffy boys in black-leather jackets milled around the front door like a flock of feeding crows, intent on their talking and smoking, barely looking up as I approached. Cigarette butts and empty Coke cans littered the cement. My old high school had had a motto over the portico: "The Truth Shall Make You Free." Here, on the bricks, someone had chalked: "Fuck Off Shithead."

I hadn't expected to open heavy glass doors like these again. Seven years of teaching had seemed like enough. That was when I had retired, to have babies, to be a housewife, to search for something new.

Inside, a secretary greeted me, handed me an armful of papers. On top I made out, "Sir Mackenzie Bowell Secondary School Teacher's

Handbook"; under it, "The Student Handbook" and three class lists. "There is more," she said. "You have some catching up to do."


It was halfway through September. I was replacing someone who couldn't "handle" her classes, someone who'd been fired.

"And how do you feel about a special school?" the principal had asked at the interview. He was a small, round man in his late fifties, his white shirt wrinkled, his wispy hair combed sideways across a pink scalp. He'd leaned forward, right to the edge of his seat, and for one moment he'd looked like Humpty Dumpty, as if what I said next could make him come tumbling down.

"A special school?" I repeated foolishly. I knew them only by reputation. They were for students in the lowest of the three "streams" in the Ontario secondary school curriculum. Near the end of the summer, when I'd first started looking for a job, I'd called one of my former colleagues for advice. "The kids at a special school will eat you alive!" he'd warned. Like so many teachers, he saw the special schools as dumping grounds, garbage bins for academic losers and hopeless behavioural cases. What he hadn't said, though we both knew it, was that I might not have a choice. There were many candidates for the available collegiate jobs, applicants whose skills were less rusty than mine.

How did I feel about a special school?

When I turned back towards the principal's intent, listening face, I weighed my words. I wanted to work; I wanted it badly. "I . . . I'd like the challenge," I lied.


The walls were grey. The couches were grey. The staff-room was a grey pool that you fell into as you turned the corner and left the shiny surfaces.

A hand emerged, a tall, thin body, beak nose, the rest of a gaunt face, as if a great, grey bird had swooped out of a cloud. He leaned over as we shook hands. "Colin Beatty, English department head." The other hand offered me a piece of paper. I glanced down. A timetable.

There were so many things I'd forgotten, and now they came flooding back: the swinging in and out of cloakroom doors; the noise of students milling in the halls; faces – yes, suddenly, the bright, receptive faces of favourite collegiate kids I'd once taught: they'd be finished university, well into their careers by now.

The department head was pointing to my timetable. Three classes, he was explaining, his voice sounding distant, disembodied: grade ten English, senior creative writing. "Home-room," I heard him add. My heart was doing such a jig that I was having trouble concentrating. Then the words, "I'll take you there."

We stood for a moment in the hall outside a classroom. On each side of the door extended a long line of dented, brown metal lockers. Through the door I heard a commotion. The department head turned. He leaned towards me, as if to communicate a secret. "There are two cardinal rules of this school that you should never forget. First, don't let yourself be vulnerable. Second, you're not going to change anything."

I was too numb to think what he meant. I watched his hand turn the knob. Before us lay turmoil: kids hanging out the window, leaning against the walls; transistor music rippling the air. It was a jumble of black-leather jackets, as if, accidentally, we had stumbled into a bikers' clubhouse.

"This is Mrs. Solnicki," the department head said, over the din. "She's taking over from Mrs. Dexter."

Momentary silence. Heads turned towards me, eyes went crafty, mouths smirked. The department head gave a fleeting smile. Then he slipped out the door.

I reached into my stunned brain and rummaged frantically for useful pedagogy. "First impressions are lasting impressions." "Never show you're nervous." "Take control immediately; once you lose it, it's hard to regain." These were principles I had acquired during teacher training, and subsequent experience had proved them true.

I squared my shoulders and took a deep breath. "May I have your attention?" I said, in what I recalled was a teacherish tone. I held the edge of the grey Formica desk so that no one would see my hands tremble. The scuffling and the rumbling continued. "May I have your attention!" I repeated firmly; my voice came out louder and higher than I would have liked, but managed to sound reasonably dignified. Still no response. "*May I have your attention, please!*" I shouted. One of the pedagogical rules, I now recalled, was "Never shout or scream. *Never, ever* shout or scream or lose your cool in any way." However, my outburst seemed to startle the students, who settled into silence. "I'm Mrs. Solnicki," I continued raspily, "and I'm going to be your home-room—"

"I haveta go to the bathroom." A tall, muscular black boy sauntered up and leaned against my desk. His hair rose steeply at the front, then sloped backward like a roof.

"I'm sorry, but you'll have to wait."

"Then I'll piss in my pants." He was standing close to me. He pursed his lips and said it into my face. The class snickered.

I dug my fingers into the desk's edge to keep my voice steady. "I'm afraid I can't let you go just yet."

He turned partly away and muttered under his breath, "Then I'll piss in your mouth."

Did he really say that?

I turned to the blackboard, wrote "SOLNICKI" in large letters.

"Sol-sol-solnic. . . . God, what kinda name is that?"

I glared at the pleased pink face framed in peroxided curls. Must take control! Now was the time. "You!" I glanced down at the seating plan. "Dori! Go to the back!"

"I will not!" This was unexpected. What pedagogy applied here?

Calm. I fought to keep my voice calm. "Then you'll have to go to the office."

"Make me! Try and make me!" She jumped to her feet, a platinum blond poured into her sweater and jeans, a tough girl right out of a B movie. She raised her fists, held them up like pink potatoes. "Come on, go for it!"

Was she challenging me to a *physical* fight? I'd never had a physical fight in my life!

The intercom button was on the wall by the door. I backed into it, pressed, shakily called for the vice-principal.

At last he was outside the door, a reassuringly square male figure in a brown suit. He knew her. She knew him. I could tell they had met often before.

From the hallway came a shout: "Snobby bitch!"


The English office was located in a small room beside the stairs leading to the second floor. "That's yours," the department head said, pointing to an oak desk, the old school type, the top scratched with initials. It and five others formed a jigsaw shape in the middle of the room. Around us climbed floor-to-ceiling shelves staggering under a haphazard array of books. I sat down at the desk. For one dizzy moment I felt that all the books might come tumbling down on me, like the pack of cards on Alice.

A ship of a woman suddenly sailed through the door. Her blouse strained against her billowing breasts, her skirt gusted about her hips like a spinnaker. "Hilda Becker," the department head said. "And this," he pointed to me, "is our new teacher, Jill Solnicki." He leaned heavily on the last name.

"Welcome to Mackenzie's bowels," the fat woman said. "You'll need intestinal fortitude to teach here." When she sighed, her bosom heaved as if buffeted by wind.

Sir Mackenzie Bowell, prime minister from 1894 to 1896. His short, pathetic stint made him an apt titular head for this institution. Colin Beatty had offered this remark just as Hilda Becker arrived. That signalled the end of the verbal tour he had just given me through the labyrinth. It was a semestered school, the change of classes occurring at the end of January. The day was divided into four periods of eighty minutes each, plus a forty-minute lunch. Teachers taught three classes. For the other period you either had a spare, or were assigned one of a number of duties. For half the day the kids took academic subjects; for the other half, commercial or technical courses. And as for the number of students attending, there were supposed to be 740 of them, the department head said, but approximately 15 to 25 per cent were absent on any given day. That's when Hilda Becker began to giggle; the giggles trailed the information like a bubbling wake. The ages of the kids? Well, they started in grade nine at fourteen or fifteen – but by the time they graduated . . . giggle . . . *if* they graduated . . . giggle . . . well, there were a few kids in the school who were over twenty . . . giggle.

He must have noticed my shock, because he leaned down and peered into my face. "You've only taught at a collegiate, haven't you?"

I nodded weakly.

Did I imagine he glanced at my cream cashmere sweater before he grinned: "Welcome to the streets!"?

What I knew intellectually was sinking in my stomach like a stone. I had left the advanced level, the university stream that was taught in the collegiates, the kids who were on their way to professions and bright futures. I'd left even the general level, that stream a notch lower, the kids who might go on to a community college. I was stuck with the kids who, after failing grade eight, were segregated into a special school. It offered them occupational courses, plus some academic courses at the basic level. My students were the lowest of the low.

As they first stepped into a special school, walls rose up around their future, as real as the bricks of the building itself.

Were the walls closing in around me, too?

"Good morning," I said nervously to the blur of faces before me in the creative-writing class. I turned to the blackboard, and, warily this time, wrote my name.

"You the new teacher?" someone asked. He was a tall boy who looked too old to be in high school. He slid down in his desk – last seat first row – and stretched his long legs provocatively. "D'jah hear what happened to Dexter?" The class tittered. "She cried! What a loser – she cried!" he repeated, to general merriment. I stared back. "So what we gonna be doin' in this class?" he added. Several chains hanging from his black-leather jacket jingled belligerently.

"Well. . . ." I was still thinking about Mrs. Dexter and her tears. Were they a trickle or a torrent?.And what had the class done to make her cry?

"So what are we gonna be doin'?" he repeated, forcing me to abandon the vision of the corner of Mrs. Dexter's skirt disappearing out the door.

"Well, actually. . . ." I'd been puzzling over that question. I'd taught writing before. All collegiate kids start in grade nine learning how to write a proper paragraph, with good sentence structure and correct grammar, and by grade twelve they are writing essays. But how did you teach something as amorphous, as peculiar, as fitful, as *creativity*? "The course is called creative writing," I said. "So I guess we'll be doing . . . writing."

Colin Beatty, my department head, had suggested I get them to write something on the first day; then I could assess their skills. I liked that idea. It meant I could sit back, postpone the inevitable, the moment when I actually had to teach them something.

But what should I ask them to write? I still had a book I had used when I taught senior collegiate classes: *What Can I Write About? 7,000 Topics for High School Students.*

That morning, as I'd flipped through it, an old feeling had come rushing back: the excitement of offering one's students a challenge, and having them respond with commitment, competence, and sometimes even artistry.

I handed out the list of topics I'd culled from the book. Under the heading "Description" was the following proposal: "Describe the earth as a little island of Creation amid the circumambient Void." The subject area entitled "Perspectives" suggested: "Use comparison/contrast to show that sometimes forward and backward, up and down, are all the same." Under "Society" I found: "Agree/disagree: To remake the world we have to start with ourselves as individuals."

That would give them plenty to choose from. "Pick one of the topics and write something about it," I said. I should have stopped when someone cried out, as if wounded: "How are we suppose to write about 'em if we can't even read 'em!"

That night I marked their writing. Where were our old friends Unity, Coherence, and Emphasis? What about topic sentences? Concluding sentences? Paragraphs, for God's sake! Some of the handwriting was illegible! I couldn't give anyone a mark higher than a D. Almost everyone got an E or an F. "Poor effort" I wrote at the bottom of most of them. Their papers had so many red marks they looked as if they were bleeding.

The reaction when I returned the exercises caught me by surprise. Several boys crumpled their work and tossed it into the waste-basket from their seats, like basketballs into a net. The older boy at the back threw his to the kid beside him, who, in a double play, batted it across the room and out the open window. A sudden anarchy had come over them, as if those Ds and Es and Fs were a key that had turned on some motor that had been waiting, warmed up. I felt as if I were standing alone on the road in front of them. My instinct was to move out of the way.

"This class sucks!" the deep voice snarled from the back. It was the older boy again – the spokesman. "I ain't doin' fuck-all in this class!"

"Watch your language here! We don't allow. . . ." In the path of his anger my voice faltered.

I leaned against a locker. I was supposed to be supervising the hall, ensuring that the students going by carried big wooden passes with a teacher's name engraved on them, visas that entitled them to travel abroad. At least half the students carried no such article, and their excuses were myriad: signing in, signing out, using the telephone, going to the office, to their lockers, to guidance, the teacher's pass was lost.

I was a timid border guard facing hostile travellers. After a while I abandoned the interrogations and leaned back against the cool metal: at least I would look as if I were doing my job. Through a crack in the door of Room 105 I could hear Hilda Becker's voice.

"I'd like to talk to you about the 'P' words," she was saying breathily. "Punctuality, Preparation, Politeness, respect for other People's Property." Each 'P' made a small explosion. From the pauses between words it seemed she was writing them on the blackboard.

"Respect – ain't that a 'R' word?" a male voice challenged.

"Very good, Claude, it *is* an 'R' word, but People and Property are 'P' words." She'd handled that supportively, she hadn't become defensive and flustered like me. "Of course, this all revolves around Personal Progress!" A longer pause indicated the flourish with which the words were chalked.

Incompetent, that's what I was. I'd had no prepared speech, no starter's pistol to whip out of my briefcase, no opening shot.


A bell rang. The harsh sound of scraping desks came through the wall, then voices, feet, reaching a crescendo, slowly dying away.

What should I do now? Essays were analytical, linear; they stretched an idea like an elastic. Maybe essay writing wasn't the route to go. But what was?

The last few mornings I'd watched a ritual around the copy of the *Toronto Sun* that I usually brought from the main office to the homeroom. After the boys gathered to leer over the Sunshine Girl, argue the merits of baseball players, and ponder their bio-rhythms, Dori would carry the abandoned newspaper to her desk. With her manicure scissors, she'd cut something out. When the class left I opened the paper. On the third-last page, bottom right corner, under the comics, a square gaped. Above it, perched precariously on the brink of the hole, the title: "Poet's Corner."

Even more peculiar: when I checked around the school at the end of the day, a square gaped at the bottom of the third-last page of every single discarded *Toronto Sun*.

What did it mean? Was it possible, I asked my department head, that these kids *liked* poetry? "That stuff's not poetry – it's simpery adolescent drivel," he answered. Over Dori's reluctant shoulder I had read a simple, rhyming verse called "Endless Love," sent in by a teenager.

Still, the incongruity of Dori, that B movie bombshell, carefully cutting, neatly folding, tenderly slipping into her purse a *poem* made me think. Maybe I should try poetry. After all, babies clapped to nursery rhymes, children chanted in the schoolyard, teenagers lived inside their songs.

I'd try poetry, but I'd make sure to lower my expectations. I'd kept a book of poems from the collegiate where I'd taught; surely *senior* basic-level students could understand grade nine poems.

I flipped through the slim volume, regretfully banishing Wordsworth, Frost, de la Mare, my dear old friends. Suddenly it jumped out: "Portrait of a Machine" by Louis Untermeyer. These kids took shop; they worked with machines. The subject would be concrete, familiar.

I made photocopies, passed them out, then began reading aloud: "What nudity as beautiful as this / Obedient monster purring at its toil; / Those naked iron muscles dripping oil. . . ."

"Hey, this about faggots?" the tall boy at the back interrupted.

I glared, then continued reading: "And the sure-fingered rods that never miss—"

"What's he doin' with his rod?" someone else called out.

"He's fingerin' it, stupid!"

I was relieved to put the poem down and get on with the questioning.

I began writing the assignment on the blackboard: "Explain the meaning of *metaphor* and *personification*. Then find examples in stanza. . . ."

A blur that caught the corner of my eye made me turn. The older boy was wrestling his smaller neighbour to the ground. Two students leaned out the back window. A girl gazed into a stand-up mirror on her desk and brushed her hair.

"Sit down," I said. "Stop fighting!" I yelled. "Put that away!" I screamed. I couldn't call the office, not again!

"Where does Beatty find these rejects?" someone said. "First Dexter, now this one."

The tall boy gave his opponent a last kick, then leaned, panting, against the back wall. "Ah, he probably picked her cuz she gave him a blow job."

A feeling of helplessness was falling over me like a big, white net. Energy leaked out my fingertips. Lucky Mrs. Dexter, who hadn't been able to "handle" her classes. And suddenly I saw the year stretching ahead, the two sides entrenched, the tops of helmets visible, the tips of bayonets. . . . And I was outnumbered! I'd never survive! Why had I taken this crummy job? If I wasn't fired soon, I might just quit!

What was I doing here, anyway? I didn't even like these kids. They weren't my kind of people.

2

■

# REJECTIONS

Colin Beatty looked across from his desk, kitty-corner to mine. Behind him loomed the bookshelves with their constant threat of avalanche. "How did your first week go?"

"Well," I began, affecting a jovial tone, although I was wrung out. "It was fine . . . except for having to be in home-room by eight forty-five, slavishly jumping to a bell every eighty minutes, sharing my class with the vice-principal's interruptions over the PA, marching up and down the corridor like a traffic cop during my spares, forcing my digestive juices into a feeding frenzy by eleven forty, and—"

"And battling rockers in black-leather jackets, right? Not to mention B-boys and skinheads thrown in for good measure." He grinned. "You've been away, you're not used to the routine yet, or this place. Some of us, of course, have had to work for a living." He exchanged a smirk with Hilda Becker, squeezed in at the telephone table.

They didn't understand – working for a living wasn't just about money. I pictured the years since my children had been in school full time. My search for something new had led to too many wanderings down midtown streets, through shops, galleries, passing the hours before and after lunch dates with friends. . . . I had to work, too.

"How are you finding your students? After all, they aren't exactly collegiate kids. Not quite *la crème de la crème*. More like *la crème de la* crap."

Hilda Becker snorted. "Just be glad you don't have Special Ed. *That's* the worst!"

I sighed. "Well, I'm . . . I'm having some problems. Actually, I don't really know what to do with them! Nothing I've tried works." Meekly I raised my eyes. "Any suggestions?"

Colin pulled open a drawer and plucked out a sheet of paper. "Here's a summary of the course of study."

It was divided by grades. My eye moved from year one, with its emphasis on punctuation and capitalization, to year two, with its concentration on sentence errors. In year three the focus was on paragraph writing and in the final year on the simple essay.

Colin Beatty leaned across his desk and fixed me with his eye. "Clear, correct sentences! Our students cannot write clear, correct sentences!" In the corner Hilda Becker nodded vigorously to the beat. "Then, if you can get them to organize those sentences into clear, concise paragraphs, you will have succeeded. In fact, we will carry you on our shoulders about the school, a laurel garland in your hair!"

I hung my head. It felt heavy. There would never be a laurel garland on it. "How do you go about teaching them that?"

"Exercises, exercises. As with learning to play the piano, or with tennis, getting better at anything requires repetition and practice. Over the years I've put all my lesson plans on overheads. The students read the questions, they write the answers. It's all there for them. I highly recommend the use of overheads."

Humbly, I nodded. "Yes, I really think our mandate," he continued, unfolding his tall frame, "is to get them to write clear, correct sentences. You will discover that they cannot do that simple thing." He towered over my chair. "They must not be loosed on the working world without that basic skill. So, keep it clear, keep it simple. And I can't say enough for overheads."

His eyes moved to the window. He began, in a stentorian voice:

> Since man from beast by words is known,
> Words are man's province, words we teach alone.
> When reason doubtful, like the Samian letter,
> Points him two ways, the narrower is the better.
> Plac'd at the door of learning, youth to guide,
> We never suffer it to stand too wide.

He stopped, looking pleased with himself. Then he glanced down at me. I hid my bewilderment behind a small, agreeable smile.

I found a box containing the transparencies for the overheads and wrote up a series of exercises from a grammar book. Run-on sentences, sentence fragments, comma splices, dangling participles, misplaced modifiers. . . . I had enough exercises, enough drilling for weeks. It felt good to know, at last, what I was doing.

I lugged the projector to class and set it up at the front. I focused it. Then I tried to focus my students.

I prayed that no one would peer through the door, see the airborne paper, the perambulating kids, and a teacher, hands helpless at her sides, silent beside the humming machine.

Just outside the pressing, hurting circle of my head I heard a voice: "Yah know why we get all the reject teachers? Cuz we're the reject students!"

I sniffled away the rest of the day. Colin Beatty looked at me oddly in the staff-room. He wondered, he said, if I was preparing to call in sick *already*. But it was tears trickling down behind my eyes, tears that, thankfully, remained invisible. To cry in front of these kids would be an irrevocable mistake, like stumbling and falling to your knees in the middle of circling wolves. What was it I had been told? Never let yourself be vulnerable.

But behind the leaky sinuses something else was pinging: "Reject. Reject." It butted against my brain. Such a bruising word – why did they use it?

Reject: from the Latin word "jacere," meaning "to throw." "To throw out, to cast off, to throw away as useless, unsatisfactory, worthless; to refuse to hear, receive, admit." That's how my Webster's dictionary defined it. And that, it seemed, was how these kids felt.

Had the school system cast them off? Had I? When I arrived with my expectations, when it was clear to them that they couldn't meet those standards, did they feel "thrown away" and "worthless"?

The essay writing . . . that had been all wrong. It was too reliant on logical thinking. That's why I'd turned to poetry. But I'd approached even it stressing the analytical. That was how I'd been trained, as a student, as a teacher. Should I undo that? Could I?

What did they need, anyway?

Maybe they were the ones who could tell me.


I wanted to say, "Let's call a truce!" I wanted to say, "Couldn't we start over again, pretend that last week didn't happen?"

I didn't know what to say. "Tell me something about yourselves," I offered timidly.

Suspicious silence. "Tell us about you, first," said the black-jacketed older boy at the back. A tactical move.

"Well. . . ." I squirmed. "What do you want to know?"

"You just startin' teachin', or somethin'?" The class tittered. I recognized that sound, the excitement of the predator on scenting prey.

"I'm new here. But," I added in a defensive rush, "I've taught before. In a collegiate."

Silence. They looked at each other.

A voice said: "Why'd you wanna come *here*?"

No choice, I silently answered.

"You married?" It was the tall, older boy again. He slid down in his seat as the class giggled.

"Yes."

"You got kids?"

I hesitated. He looked almost evil in his black-leather jacket and chains, his ragged hair half hiding his face. What if he intended to harm my children? He looked as if he could do that. But the entire class was waiting for my answer, as if this was somehow crucial. "Yes," I admitted in a low voice.

"How many?"

Lower. "Two."

"Boys or girls?"

"One of each." It was barely audible.

"How old?"

"Youngish," I said evasively.

"So we gonna keep doin' this crap? Dexter did this shit, too." He was an aggressive creep, but at least he'd changed the subject.

"Well, the course *is* creative writing, so, we'll, ah, obviously, we'll be . . . writing." I paused, took the plunge. "How about poetry?" I blurted.

The response was a torrent. "That *shit?*"

"You mean that rhymin' crap?"

"Faggots do that!"

"I'm transferrin'!"

I took a deep breath. "Listen, it's *creative* writing. That means you can write, well . . . whatever *you* want!" I walked down the outside row, and stopped beside a girl with a dyed-blond streak in her dark hair, her jersey covered in writing. The line across her breasts said: "THERE ARE LOTS OF THINGS I LIKE ABOUT YOU, BUT I CAN'T PUT MY FINGER ON THEM." "That's writing," I said. Now I had come to my interrogator in the last seat. How old was he? Nineteen? Twenty? His face, close up, looked ravaged, as if those years had been lived hard. On his T-shirt, under his black jacket, I could make out: "IF YOU AIN'T A BIKER, YOU AIN'T SHIT." "Look, you can even write on skin." I pointed to the tattoo of a skull on the back of his hand, "F.T.W." engraved underneath. "What does that mean?" I asked.

He smiled, exposing yellow teeth. "The last two words are 'the world'."

I looked around for help in guessing the first word. "It's four letters," he offered, and the class howled.

"So you see, writing can be anything!" I said quickly, feeling the heat rise in my face. "That's why," I took another breath, *"creative* writing is . . . *fun!"*

Five rows of eyes stared sceptically. "Let's try a game," I added quickly, hoping to catch them off guard, disarm them. "Open up your minds. Whatever comes in, write it down. Whatever it is, we'll call it poetry!" I raced to the front, grabbed foolscap from the pile on the desk.

Grumbling, muttering, followed by silence, long glassy stares. Finally, the girl with the blond streak lowered her head. Another head followed. Pencils moved across paper. Now, only the sound of scratching.

"I don't have nuthin' to say," a fat boy at the front whined. "I never was no good in English."

"Then write about how you have nothing to say!" He looked as startled by my answer as I was. Then a light blinked in his face. Down went his head.

"*Anything* you want. *Any way* you want," I repeated softly, softly, as I walked up and down the aisles. The words felt foreign, an abandoning of control, as if I were inviting them to rise up, their sharpened pencils raised in their hands, to plunge the lead tips into my heart, saying: "You gave us permission? This is what we really want." But the pencils were busy scratching on paper, and my intact, surprised heart beat an accompaniment.

Poems fluttered down to my desk. I looked at the pile, astounded that it had grown from such odd, vague instructions.

"I'd like to read these aloud," I said. A howl of protest erupted.

Why had I said that? These small outpourings were the first tentative steps across No Man's Land. I could jeopardize these gains, send the kids running for cover. "Suppose" – I looked around – "I don't mention names?"

The girl with the blond streak nodded. I was encouraged. I separated a piece of wrinkled, blotchy foolscap from the others.

> life is shit
> I wish I could quiet
> there has been days
> when the earth just caves
> in and leaves you there
> I just grin and bare I just
> stand there to be put down agian.

"Your poem was very honest, Jack," I murmured, glancing down at the seating plan to fix his name in my mind. I placed it on his desk. It had been so raw that I hardly knew what to say. He stared straight ahead, his thin back rigid, his pale face screwed into a scowl.

I rallied. "Let's play some games." Maybe the trick to creative writing was to feel free – it had worked the first time. "We're going to do free association. I'll say a word, and you answer with the first thing that comes into your head."

"*Anything?*" said the tattooed boy. He bared his sharp yellow teeth. *Ray . . . Ray . . . mantaray.* I worked his name into my memory.

"Well. . . . Within the bounds of what's acceptable in a classroom, of course." But what exactly was that? Since I'd made the decision to reject my expectations rather than my students, what *were* the guidelines? Uncertainly I turned back to the game. "The word 'creep' reminds you of . . . ?"

"Snails."

"Bugs."

Jack's poem had been so startling, so unlike anything a student had ever handed me before, that, in spite of his reaction to my overture, I couldn't help sneaking glances in his direction. His hair was faded red, his face expressionless. He held a stubby pencil, while his other hand lay, white and open, on the paper. Under the desk his sneakers sat together and his knees fell apart. Somewhere beneath that limpness surged the despair and fury that had charged his poem.

"Jack?"

There was a pause. "Teacher," came back almost inaudibly.

"Hmm . . . okay," I said, determinedly cheerful. "Now let's try another game. Someone start a sentence, then someone else finish it. For example: First the cocoon, then the butterfly."

"First the engagement," the girl with the blond streak called out.

"Then the break-up," another girl finished.

"First the party," said a small boy in the second row.

"Then the cops," Ray concluded.

"First the world," someone else began.

Silence. I turned towards that pale, strained face. "Jack? Can you finish it?"

"First the world," he repeated softly, reluctantly. "Then the war."

3

## JACK'S POEM

"Fuckin' asshole!" exploded into the fresh morning air of the parking lot on this crisp, sunny Monday, my third Monday at school. Kids faced each other, then moved slowly apart. A door slammed. A rusty car with no plates roared out of a parking spot, spewing exhaust. It raced down the driveway, barely missing a teacher-driven Honda, then lurched onto the road.

He passed me in the hall – alone, staring straight ahead.
"Hi, Jack," I said, friendly.
He didn't move his face. But his hand rose slightly, before it fell.

I had tried to teach the class metaphor and personification the day I presented the poem about the machine, but they had refused to listen. Was it the words themselves, strutting about like pompous executives stuffed into their vests? But imagery was a bedrock of poetry – it should be taught.

If they felt like rejects, then their self-esteem was wanting. In the book *One Hundred Ways to Achieve Self-Esteem*, I found an exercise called "IF I COULD BE . . ." It reminded me of the Let's Pretend games of childhood. Might it help set free their imaginations?

To understand metaphor and personification, they needed to see that things can slide, shift, change place, take on disguises.

They handed in the written answers:

1. If I could be a animal I wouldnt, because the way I am is just fine with me, and Im not doin this shit its stupid. (Ray)
2. If I cud be a bulding Id be this school so I cud burn my self down. (Jack)
3. If I could be a piece of furniture I'd be a chair so girls would sit on my face.
4. If I could be a colour I'd be white because it outstanding colour. (A black girl)

As happy as. . . . As colourful as. . . . The point of the next set of exercises was for them to complete the phrases with something original.

I walked up and down the aisles, silently reading:

As colourful as puke after a pizza.
As fresh as virgin pussy.
As sad as a empty-handed thief.

I passed Jack's desk. He was writing with that stubby pencil, his hand cramped around it like a claw. I offered him the one I was carrying, sleek and brightly yellow. He growled something that sounded like, "Don't want it."

I glanced down. The words jumped off his page. In large, black letters he'd scrawled: "I WISH THIS CLASS WOULD JUST DIE."

An icy wave of fear washed over me.


As I was reading the next set of poems aloud – keeping the writers anonymous, of course – I kept darting looks at the desk in the far row, by the window. Jack was leaning forward, his face pink, his small ears perked like a fox's.

He wanted me to read his poem, I could tell. But I was still weighing what to do. I finished another poem, this one written by a girl with a long braid who kept something called the *Good News Bible* open on her desk.

Jack's poem loomed up, a smudge of heavy writing, as if he had bludgeoned the paper with a charcoal bat. Would I be encouraging the same sentiments and language from the others if I read it? And what would it do to their image of me when they heard me say . . .

> School is a drag somedays,
> most other days it's a down
> right bore do know some
> of the teachers are good but
> some of them are BLOODY
> GREAT PRICKS
> and should be thrown out
> of the fucken school!

Anxiously I looked around, at loud laughing mouths, at wide eyes. The class was surprised. But something else: appreciative.

"Have things improved in your creative writing class since you introduced the overheads?" Colin Beatty's craggy face wore an almost paternal expression.

I'd been waiting for this. I cleared my throat nervously. "Well, I don't know. Maybe it's me, but . . . I just couldn't get the kids to work on them. Actually, I'm moving in a . . . a different direction from Mrs. Dexter."

"Oh?" He leaned across the desk, his tall frame hunched.

"It *is* writing." I cleared my throat again. "It's . . . poetry." The word fell with a thud.

He jumped up suddenly. "My dear, inexperienced, teacher-not-of-special-schools-born, I don't think you should go off on your own, half-cocked! First, you don't know what our students' needs are. Second, your former teaching took place in a completely different setting. Third, you were retired for a *very* long time . . ." – he paused significantly – "and may be quite out of touch with current methodology."

"But, actually, they're writing some interesting . . . *stuff*." I avoided the word "poetry."

"Clear sentences!" he interjected in a rising voice. "Clear, correct sentences!" He moved to the bookshelves. "Listen not just to me, but to the experts." Under a pile of papers he found what he was looking for. He

flashed the title at me: *Teaching the Slow Learner in the Secondary School.*
He drew himself to his full height and quoted sonorously:

> Dull children have few talents to help them lead "full"
> lives. The idea of everyone being naturally endowed with
> some gift is not borne out by the experience of those who
> work with the dull. Dull children are backward in every-
> thing. They might be better at manual skills than they are
> at academic subjects, but their ability is relative. They are
> still not as good as bright children. No skill comes easily,
> imagination is often limited.

"My dear Jill." He shook his head back and forth; gaunt, in his grey
cardigan, he looked like a heron holding a squirming fish in its beak.
"Poetry is an activity utilizing the imagination. They *cannot* write poetry!
Nor is it what they *need*! Remember, this is *not* a collegiate. Didn't I tell
you the two cardinal rules of the school? First, you're not going to change
anything. Second. . . ."

I raised my eyes, puzzled. I'd been impressed by what my students
had handed in. "Well, what is it you think they *are* capable of?"

"Thank you. Thank you for asking that question." His voice had taken
on the exasperated tone of a teacher whose student is missing the core of
the lesson. He flipped to another page, quoted again:

> Imaginative written compositions or essays cannot be
> expected of a really dull child, and they will see little
> purpose in them, but they can be taught to write simple,
> straightforward paragraphs on things they have learnt or
> seen or heard.

He closed the cover with a loud clap. "You'll find this book here any
time you need it."

Our national anthem wafted sluggishly through my restless home-room
class, over Dori, her shapely bum cupped in tight jeans. Breasts pushed

provocatively under her sweater; peroxided curls framed a pouty, impudent mouth. A few weeks ago she had been the one who'd called me a snobby bitch.

"I'm bein' charged with assault," she said, after the anthem, showing me a cut on her inside lip. She rolled her eyes. They were so weighted with mascara I wondered how she could move them. "I was on the bus last night, there were three boys, makin', you know, comments. I told 'em to screw off. They jumped me, tore my blouse."

"Why are *you* charged?"

"I stabbed one of 'em in the arm. He had to get stitches. Cops told me he's layin' charges. That's when I really started screamin'. They're chargin' *me* with assault? They tore *my* blouse! I'll charge *them!*" She reached into her purse and pulled out a knife. I flinched. But the hilt curled peacefully in her palm, harmless as a sleeping snake. I was even able to admire its oak and brass trim, the way, not approaching too near, you might admire a snake's patterned back.

Jamie's obese form was wedged into his desk's seat. He pried himself loose to give the knife a closer inspection. "That's illegal," he pronounced.

"It ain't! If the blade fits in the palm of your hand you're okay. I hid it in the garbage." She smiled smugly. "Police never found it."

"Well!" A comment seemed expected of me. "I don't think you should carry a knife." Her mouth began to curl defiantly. I glanced at the intercom, in case someone was listening, and lowered my voice. "But I have to admit you were gutsy to fight back. I'm sure *I* wouldn't have had the nerve!"

A short time ago those pink fists had been raised against me. Since then they'd turned against others. She was only fifteen, maybe sixteen, and so tough!

Her face flushed. She smiled.


Jack was waiting at the classroom door when I arrived. That surprised me. Every time I looked in his direction his gaze dropped to the desk, or slid towards the window. He followed me in. "I'll take that pencil," he said softly. His pale blue eyes met mine, then bounced away. His face coloured red as his hair.

"Okay." I smiled back uneasily – I hadn't forgotten his death threat to the class. "But I need collateral." Most of the kids came to class without paper, pen, or pencils, and borrowed equipment frequently went unreturned. Hilda Becker had advised me to ask for security when I made a loan.

Jack reached into his back pocket and pulled out a wallet. Something clattered to the floor. I bent down, picked up the heavy handle – black, inlaid with steel. Automatically my thumb pressed the button. Out lunged a blade, shocking as a hissing tongue.

Tensely I handed it back. He snapped it shut and shoved it into his pocket. He saw my wide eyes: a smile lurked around his mouth.

He lingered awkwardly in front of me, then abruptly picked the wallet off the desk, opened it, and offered several photographs: images of the militia marching at Old Fort York. They wore ceremonial blue costumes; over their shoulders they carried muskets. One thin soldier was Jack.

"You in the militia?" Ray called from across the room. He swaggered over, his motorcycle boots clicking on the linoleum. "Why're you dressed like *that?*"

Jack turned. "For the lieutenant-governor. He reviewed us." His voice was a whisper.

"What kinda gun you use?"

"Flintlock musket."

"You shoulda blown the ol' guv'ner away." Ray grinned his yellow grin.

Jack studied him cooly. "No ammunition. Anyhow, he was too far away."

"Next time carry a three fifty-seven Magnum, then do it. What a rush!"

Jack stared. Around the photographs his long white fingers curled.

4

## WHAT AM I DOING HERE?

The headache crept in on tiptoe, then marched in boots. I fled to the women's washroom to gulp Aspirins, then raced down the hall and arrived late for my grade ten English class. They were milling around at the back. One of the shaggy-haired troublemakers had his leg out a window as if to make his getaway.

Mr. Pritchett, a geography teacher, burst through the door. "*Your students* are pounding on the walls! I am trying to do a soil profile in the next room and *your students* are going crazy!" His small eyes darted, his sharp nose twitched. "Punctuality" – he gave me a particularly pointy look – "is something we're trying to teach!" He spun around and whisked out.

I turned to the class. "Can't I be a few minutes late without worrying that you're out of control?" What had happened to them? They'd started off well-behaved, but this last week they'd gotten more and more restless. The office was still changing timetables and moving kids around; at the beginning of the week a new girl, Christie, had transferred in. It was her fault; she was always provoking me. The class had been fine before her.

The escape artist, Kevin – I'd learned his name quickly because he was so troublesome – edged back towards the window. "Sit down!" I yelled.

"Referral, Referral, send him to Referral," the boy beside him sang. I'd sent *him* down yesterday. Before Christie came, I hadn't sent anybody to Referral Room, home of the Kicked-Out. You had to signal the office first, and it was embarrassing to do it too often.

"Send me to Referral," Kevin chimed. He scrunched his pimply face into a mocking grin.

"All right! You're going!" The bile was stinging my throat.

Where were the forms? Were they the blue ones or the pink ones? Nurse excuse slips were white, Library permits pink. I grabbed a sheet of foolscap from the drawer, scrawled, "Referral Room" on it.

From outside the door came the sound of paper crumpling. I ran out, catching up with Kevin halfway down the hall. He opened his fist; my orders were a tight ball, my signature obliterated. "Give me that!" I croaked. Across the creases I wrote: "STUDENT CRUMPLED PAPER!! MUST NOT RETURN FOR TWO DAYS!!!" He resumed his jaunty walk, a boy whistling on a journey that did not look as if it led to the Referral Room.

"Hello? Hello?" The office was calling me back. I was just in time to hear the intercom click off.

"They're gone, miss," someone said. "They gave up." It was Clive, a small, wiry black boy, speaking from under a high, squared box of hair.

"Miss, are you havin' problems at home?" he asked.

"No! I'm having problems with this class!"


The long face inserted itself through the crack in the door. "I had a Polaroid camera in my cupboard," Mr. Pritchett hissed. "I left the room empty for a few minutes and now it's gone." His eyes got narrower. "It must be one of your students. You left them in your class unsupervised."

I had come to the class during change of period, unlocked the door, then gone to make a phone call. Several kids had come into the room while I was out.


At the three o'clock bell, Clive peered around the door of the English office, his eyes round. His hair seemed even stiffer, from tension. "I know who took the camera!" he whispered urgently. "Kevin took it! I saw him sneak into Pritchett's room. He put it under his jacket, then took off to his locker." His eyes grew rounder. "Don't let anyone know I told!" He disappeared.

What was I supposed to do?

The wide-eyed face returned. "Kevin's just outside!"

He wanted me to *do* something.

I could see the back of a navy jacket partway down the path winding between the pines. He was heading towards the road, a bus, freedom. He swung a grey duffel bag.

"Kevin?" I called. He turned. "Come here." Friendly. I was friendly.

He exchanged a glance with his buddy. His buddy took the bag.

"Bring your bag, too," I added pleasantly.

He was coming towards me!

"Mr. Pritchett told me he's, well . . . he's missing something from the cupboard in his class. A camera." A look of alarm crossed his face. I was encouraged. "Several of you were in the class before I came. So I'm afraid I have to . . . check out all of you." I gave a weak smile. "Just in case."

"I took it," he said. "It's in my bag."

Did criminals confess so readily? I had an urge to take the camera and run. "Well then, I guess I'll . . . have to take you to Mr. Taggert." Should I grab his arm? But he walked, compliant beside me, down the hall into the vice-principal's office.

Five o'clock. Two policemen were questioning Kevin. The officer with the broad face and turned-up nose was barely out of his teens; it was the black military boots and yellow nub of a walkie-talkie poking from his pocket that lent him the illusion of years. The other cop had a moustache and hair combed sideways to cover his bald spot.

"So why'd yah take the camera? Were yah bored, or what?"

Shrug. Kevin's face was pale, tired.

"You ever been in trouble with the law before?"

"He's got a record," the baby-faced cop said.

"You wanna tell me about that?" The bully flexed in the balding policeman's voice.

As if on cue, Kevin's voice altered too, its edges sharpening with his legal rights. "I don't haveta answer that!"

"What d'yah have in your pockets?"

Kevin stood up, thin and straight, and produced a pen (mine, I noted), a hairbrush, and some change. He slapped them down on the table, fleshing out the new role.

"Take off yer jacket!" Their fingers slipped under the waistband of his jeans, their hands slid down the inside of his thighs. I looked away, shocked at this trespass.

"Where'd yah get this jacket? Down, isn't it?"

Silence.

"Answer when we talk to yah!" Even the younger policeman's voice had deepened.

"Yeah."

"Yes, sir!"

"Yes, sir," Kevin muttered to his feet.

The balding cop put the pen and hairbrush into his pocket. "Don't want someone with somethin' sharp sittin' behind me in the car. Unless you want handcuffs on." He smirked at his partner.

And now the transformation was complete. Kevin, staring straight ahead, arms loosely hanging, was marched out the door, past me, past the weary vice-principal slumped in his chair. A convict between his guards.

I followed into the front foyer, watching through the windows as he disappeared inside the back seat of the shiny cruiser.


"Oh God, what have I done?" I cried out to the blotchy face that stared back from the mirror in the women's washroom. "I've sent someone to jail!" I looked around desperately as if the humming fluorescent lights or the two empty cubicles might offer an answer to the question. "What am I doing here?"


"Jill?" Colin Beatty cleared his throat. He folded his frame awkwardly as he sat. He didn't fit his desk any better than I fit in this school.

"Mr. Pritchett" – the name jolted me from my daze – "has been complaining that the noise from your junior English class interrupts his teaching. He says the class seems a little . . ." – he coughed – "out of control. Apparently, a theft occurred while you were out of the room." I opened my mouth to protest that the camera had been returned. He raised a finger. "Just remember: 'Good fences make good neighbours.'" Even Robert

Frost was being conscripted against me.

The paternal expression reappeared. I grew warier. "I realize that you've not been here long, and it *is* an adjustment – everyone takes that into account." He lifted his hand, fingers splayed, as if giving a benediction. "But if I may read to you from the Good Book again. . . ." Head bowed like a preacher, he opened *Teaching the Slow Learner in the Secondary School.*

I sat, too numb to catch more than a few phrases: "social adequacy," "respect for adults," "respect for authority."

He put down the book and stared meaningfully at me while, inside my head, the refrain thudded: What am I doing here?


"White boy!"

I stopped in the middle of the front foyer as if I'd heard a shot.

"Fuck you!" It was Ray. He too had stopped. He faced the two black boys who leaned against the floor-to-ceiling windows. Outside milled the smokers, inhaling their last drags before school started.

"What you say, mother-fucker?" The muscular black boy's big hand shot out and slammed against Ray's chest, jangling the chains on his jacket. "I'm gonna kick your ass, white meat!" He showed his teeth.

Ray's mouth curled. "Kick this, nigger!" Foot exploded into groin. The boy folded to his knees. The second boy hurtled forward like a missile, catching Ray in the gut, crashing him against the wall.

But I was more than a stunned spectator; I was a teacher. Shouldn't I *do* something? Shouldn't I insert myself between those two bodies, make it three?

I sidled over. "Hey, guys," I said timidly. No response. Tentatively I placed my hand on Ray's wrist, just above the tattoo. "Get yer fuckin' hands off me!" he snarled, eyes glued to his opponent. I withdrew my arm in a hurry. Fingers grabbed Ray's jersey, stretched it like gum. "Guys . . . ," I pleaded. A punch flew past my head! Another! I looked up into sweaty, panting faces, clenched teeth. The grey silk of my blouse seemed a fragile armour.

The burly form of the machine-shop teacher suddenly cut in front of me. Other arms reached in. Now five or six pairs of hands pulled on each boy – a tug-of-war.

The battlers were wrenched apart. The momentum threw Ray to the other side of the foyer where more hands clutched at him. He began to wrestle with someone who'd grabbed his leg. By now trailing a length of kids like a kite ribbon, he raised his fist at the two black boys: "You're fuckin' dead, niggers!"

Mr. Taggert, the vice-principal, came huffing down the hall, suit jacket flapping, red hair springing out from his head. The crowd that had pressed in through the front door untied its large, excited knot. Limping, the boys were led down to the office.

I'd never seen anything like this. Prejudice, yes, but of a slyer, more evasive kind, slipping in then out of a room, so that you saw it but then doubted your perceptions.

But there was no doubting this *hate* that was nourished on skin colour. And I'd stood helpless, unable to stop it.

I stared at my shaking hands.

5

■

# HOW WAS YOUR WEEKEND?

For several weeks the home-room bunch had sniffed me out the way dogs do, making forays to the front, warily friendly. And I had been making an effort to reciprocate. A policy of openness was working with the creative-writing class, where more were handing in poems, wanting to hear them read. I was trying it here, too.

"How was your weekend?" I asked.

"You shoulda seen it at the courtroom!" Leroy chortled, interrupting his pacing in front of the window. Leroy liked to be up at the front – that's where he'd been four weeks ago on my first day, rudely insisting that he had to go to the bathroom. "Sean was there. Kevin was there. Randy was there. Everyone from Bowell was at one end, like a family!" He comically contorted his face. "Got a suspended sentence, forty hours' community work." Long-legged, loose, like the track star I'd been told he was, he bounded to the door and back, graceful as an antelope.

I pushed aside my timetables. From 8:45 until the bell rang at 9:10 there was only the national anthem to preside over. "What did you do?"

"Got caught shopliftin'."

"At Woolco?" Gus asked.

"Naw, don't shoplift there no more. Scarborough Town Centre."

"What'd *you* do, half-breed?" Jamie said to his neighbour Sean, a light-skinned black boy.

Sean sat collapsed in his seat, as if he hadn't the strength to hold himself up. "You know that stabbin' at Riviera Court? She come crawlin' downstairs, bleedin' all over the place. I was alone cuz my mom's on the night shift."

"Yer mom's a hooker!" Jamie crowed.

"No she ain't – she's a nurse. I had to go to court, testify against the guy." He laid his head back down on the desk as if it were a pillow.

"I know that girl!" Dori said. "She has long hair, right? A coupla kids, one on the way? I saw her at the beer store this summer. Her boyfriend made her use her last two dollars to buy beer. That fuckin' bastard pulled her hair! I'da punched him out if I was her!" Her shadow-heavy eyes flashed.

"I saw a guy bein' shot at my place," John announced from the door. He walked bowlegged in his tight jeans, as if he'd just dismounted. "A Rastafarian. There was guys in a Cadillac shoutin', 'Where's the drugs?' I heard 'bam'! It was great!"

Jamie looked up at me. They all turned. "So what'd you do on your weekend, miss?"


"See me." The note from Mr. Taggert, the vice-principal, was in my mailbox, second row, fifth across, in the main office. What had I done? Nervously I walked past the line of kids and tapped on his door. It opened suddenly and someone barged out. "Hi, Ray." I moved back to avoid the metal spikes bristling from his wristband.

Mr. Taggert was sitting behind a large desk. It was only 9:30, but already his tie was loosened, sleeves rolled up, strands of reddish hair flying around his face. The desk was a Sargasso Sea, choked with pink Referral Room forms, small patches of brown wood gasping for air. On the wall hung a picture of two attractive, clean-cut boys, and beside it one of those huge calendars that show a year. The weeks piled up – big, white, teetering blocks.

"I just wanted to tell you that you handled that camera business nicely," he said.

"I did?" I felt behind me for the chair. "But . . . I was the one that caused it to happen in the first place." The pang returned.

"Who told you that? Believe me, there were thefts in this place long before you arrived! You did an excellent job of getting the camera back."

"Really? Well, thank you." I let out a long sigh, the sound of an over-filled balloon after its neck has been unknotted. "But what's going to happen to Kevin? Will he go to jail?"

"Oh, probably he'll just get a warning."

"But he'll be expelled!" I had been feeling terrible.

He glanced down at the swarm of pink sheets. "I've suspended him for a couple of days. I must tell you," he added, seeing my surprise, "that I am very reluctant to expel kids. It's against my philosophy of education for the special schools. After all, where can they go if *we* won't take them in? As well," – he shuffled paper – "when we lose students, we lose jobs. Each student is one-twelfth of a teacher."

The slight boy with the shock of dark hair dropped the Transfer Slip on my desk and indicated where I should sign. Grudgingly, I scratched my initials, admitting him to my junior English class. I didn't want another student this far into the term.

"Take a seat," I said glumly. The front desks were empty, the kids congregating as far back as possible, as if I breathed contagion. David stood uncertainly, then took the desk directly opposite mine. He raised his face, eyes dark with mauve undershadows, and smiled tentatively.

Because I'd asked the others in the class to write brief autobiographies when I started, I asked the new boy for one too.

#### ABOUT ME

> My name is David Blane and I am 15 years old. I have had my share of problems with family, school and law. Last year I got suspended eleven times. Finaly I was kicked out until I could get control of myself and conker my problem of my bad temper – once I start I can't stop! But things are going great so far this year. I cleaned up my act and I'm STAYING CLEAN.

"The concluding sentence is really important," I said to the junior English class. "You want to make your point strongly." I was teaching the paragraph using Colin Beatty's guidelines – "simple, straightforward paragraphs on things they have learnt or seen or heard."

Clive, the wiry black boy, the Informer, spoke up. "I know what you mean, miss. You want to whip it out and wave it around!" He turned to Milos, a soft-eyed Greek boy with a shy grin above a white shirt and grey sweater vest. "Hey," he poked him in the stomach. "You eatin' too much spaghetti, Milos."

"Yeah," someone else chimed. "Your ma's cookin' too much chow mein."

I hesitated, debating whether to guide the class back to concluding sentences, chastise the racist slur, or correct the information on ethnic foods.

"He's been beatin' his meat in the washroom," someone cut in, still on the food theme.

"Slammin' the ham." Maybe they hadn't eaten breakfast.

"Pinchin' the inch." Milos laughed too.

"They caught Catnapper in the library again," someone yelled.

"Catnapper?" I said.

"Little niner, goes behind the shelves where Mr. Walpole keeps them big picture books. Shoots his load."

"Yeah, he goes to the library to get a grip on himself." Everyone laughed.

"Masturbation," I interjected, "is a perfectly normal physical and emotional—"

"In the *library*, miss?"

"She sounds like Dr. Ruth!"

I turned around. Someone had gotten into the class before me. Now sex came in the guise of a poem, floating in the middle of the empty blackboard.

> **The cockeyed**
> **girl with**
> **dark red hair**
> **dances on the edge of**
> **Milos dream.**

"Who wrote that?"

Clive put up his hand.

"It's wonderful!" I gave him the special, intimate smile reserved for those with whom you share a secret. "So, who's the cockeyed girl with red hair?" I smiled again.

He pointed at her, that girl, my enemy – Christie.

All eyes turned. "Why's it good to be an egg?" she said loudly. "First, because yah get laid, second, because yah get eaten, third. . . ."

"That's enough!" I snapped.

But she continued. "It useta be, two years ago, if yah said you were a virgin, people said, 'Oh, God, go out and lose it tonight, girl!' Now they say, 'Hey, good for you!'"

Before I could stop her she'd strutted to the front and scrawled a debate topic on the board: Should a Girl Be a Virgin When She Marries?

The Yea's, sitting on the right, spoke first.

"I want my wife to be a virgin when she gets married cuz it'd be more exciting for her."

Interruption from the negative: "Hey, you never got your dinky stinky?"

David, turning around from his seat at the front: "It'd be nice to be able to please a woman who hasn't been around with every Tom, Dick, or Harry."

Interruption from the negative: "Especially every hairy dick!"

Clive: "I wouldn't want a woman who's had sex more than five or six times."

Christie: "Five times, or five different men? There's a difference." She wore tight jeans, heavy make-up, her hair was dyed red, she sounded as if she *knew* the difference. Yet, for some reason, she was sitting with the pro-virgins.

Clive, clarifying his point: "Five times. Like, right now there's no way I'd want a virgin; but when I get married, I want one."

Quiet kid in the corner: "I come from a old-fashioned family—"

Interruption from the negative: "He's from a farm, he does it with the cows. Moo. . . ."

". . . and . . . and . . . a woman should be a virgin, to prove she loves you. But a man should be experienced so he can give maximum pleasure."

"Like the hands just ain't good enough, honey!" Christie said, author-itative but virginal.


Then the Nays, on the left.

"I don't want on my weddin' night a woman who doesn't know what she's doin'."

"Yeah, who wants a dead lay on your weddin' night?"

Interruption from Clive: "Teach her! Unless you don't know what *you're* doing!"

Cammy, a fat, shy girl in the last seat: "You know that person that said a girl should be a virgin to prove her love? Well, if the boy isn't a virgin, how do you know he loves you?"

Nadine, a pretty blond girl with dangling earrings: "Um, well. . . ."

Clive, spinning around: "Um, well. . . ." His tongue darted out.

"It hurts," she continued, turning pink. "She shouldn't be in pain on her wedding night."

Christie, authoritatively: "Most people get so pissed they pass out on their weddin' night. They do it in the morning."

Only one person hadn't spoken: Milos, alone and undecided in the middle row.

Clive: "What d'you think, Milos?"

Milos: "I dunno."

Clive: "You dunno? You dunno? You dunno what sex is!"


Later, I looked up from the newspaper to find Mr. Pritchett crouched on his haunches beside me. His smile was conciliatory. "At first I thought something terrible was happening in your room! That's why I came run-ning to your door, to help you."

I scanned the staff-room but no one was listening. The few people there were reading, or playing bridge, or doing crossword puzzles from the newspaper.

"Thanks, but I was just fine! We were, ah, examining certain social issues relating to sex-role designation in our culture."

His eyes narrowed suspiciously.

"Listen, I'm sorry if they bothered you. I admit they were noisy. But it was a really good discussion. Debate, actually!" I could feel the pleasure rekindling – because a debate had been taking place. With these kids! "Actually," I beamed down at him, "I think it was the very best class we've had!"

"Oh. Well, I'm sure you must do some quiet seat work, too." He scrambled awkwardly to his feet as Hilda Becker lowered herself into the chair beside me.

"How's it going?"

"Things seem to be improving!" I announced.

Her knowing smile said: Let's just wait and see.


The motley crew was in home-room. I use the term advisedly: two of the boys were wearing MÖTLEY CRÜE T-shirts, Jamie's large stomach stretching the band's name to billboard proportions.

John sat on the top of his desk. "Pritchett's fuckin' failin' me already." Painfully he unhitched his legs. John wore the same skin-tight black jeans every day, his fly partly unzipped like a mouth gasping for air. Under an outer leather jacket and an inner jean jacket, he wore the same black jersey, cut high above the waist, his belly button exposed. Like a plunging neckline, was it meant to suggest other possibilities?

"He's been buggin' me too," Dori said angrily. "If he phones my mom like last year, I'm gonna vandalize his car so bad!" She paused. "I'd do it, too! I did it to Mrs. Wheeton." She looked at me for a reaction.

"What did you do?" I complied, sipping my coffee.

"Kicked in her doors, spray-painted her car, knifed the tires. She was my principal in public school." She looked pleased.

"Bust the front and back windows," Gus suggested. "That's seven hundred dollars."

Leroy interrupted his pacing in front of the window. "Put sugar in the gas tank." He stared out the window, past the pines, to the flaming maple near the road. Lithe, taut, a caged black panther.

"Get rid of his car," John suggested. "My father'll do it for yah."

"My old man handles hot stuff, jewellery. . . ," Jamie interrupted, shifting his bulk off the desk. "Flip through the Consumers' catalogue. I can get anything for yah. He knows people – knows the godfather of all Canada!" He looked around to see if anyone was listening.

"I guarantee my dad can get you any car made in Canada in the last six weeks for a thousand bucks," John rolled on.

"How can he?" I took another sip of coffee.

"Just change the serial number and . . . a few other things." He smiled mysteriously.

"What does your father do for a living?" It was a comfortable question, the question I had often asked other children when I was growing up. The answer unlocked a lifestyle: the size of your house, whether you went on ski holidays, or trips to the Caribbean. It was the question one always got around to because it contained all other questions, all other answers.

He tossed his thin blond hair. "Tow-truck operator."

The vice-principal's voice boomed over the PA: "May I have your attention, please! A blue 1985 Renault is missing from Shop 13. Anyone with information regarding this incident should see Mr. Taggert as soon as possible in the front office!"

6

■

# A QUESTION OF RACE

Christie barged into junior English class late and slammed the door. "You've missed three days of work," I muttered, my lesson interrupted.

"But it's so boring. I'm sorry to say this, but it's sooo boring! Those stupid little paragraphs on what we learnt and seen and heard on the way to school." Tall and slinky, she leaned against the blackboard. "So show me what I missed." She picked up a piece of chalk and drew the "C" of her name, large, snakey, insistent. The "H" and "R" and "I" slithered after. She made a big production of the "S" for her audience.

"Let's get back to the book," I growled. They were supposed to be quietly reading – although most talked or passed notes. The novel was about a homeless boy. I had just compared the hero to a stray dog. "You don't see many strays in Toronto," I added, as an afterthought.

"That's 'cause the Humane Society picks 'em up and kills 'em," Christie called, on the way to her seat.

"True. In poorer countries like, say, Mexico, you see so many skinny strays, wandering, eating garbage." On my travels they made me sad, the furtive dogs, the shadow cats. The children who lived among them.

"Yeah, like the Chinks," she said.

"Pardon?"

"There's so many of 'em. Breedin'."

"Yeah, same's with the guys in the turbans. They're always pushin' when yah get in front of 'em," someone else said.

"Who?"

"Pakis."

"Diapers on their heads."

"They're so dirty, miss!"

"They stink!"

"They worship cockroaches!"

"They brought cockroaches into our building. And they live twenty people in a room! Alls yah smell in the halls is their cookin'!"

"And that push-button in the middle of their forehead? Like, if they don't accept our ways, why don't they go back home?" Christie tossed her red mane.

"Yeah, all them people from other countries, they're takin' our jobs."

"Our jobs and our women," Kevin added, back after his brief suspension.

"Soon's they come over here they go on welfare, sit on their asses," Christie said.

"Get free houses and cars and money so there's nothin' left for us."

"Yeah, and we're the ones been here longer."

"I'd stop people on the street," Kevin said. "If they didn't speak English I'd shoot 'em!"

"Put 'em in a boat in the middle of the Atlantic, torpedo it!"

"Those blacks, they don't do nothin'! Then they drive around in Cadillacs!" Christie said.

"Hey, I don't have a Cadillac!" Clive twisted around in his seat. Everyone ignored him.

"There's no one in Jamaica cuz all of 'em are here."

"Yeah, send 'em all back where they come from!"

"Wait a minute!" I held up my hand like a policeman trying to stop a speeding car. "Aren't we *all* immigrants?" I turned to Kevin. "For example, where are your parents from?"

"England. That's different."

"What's the difference," Christie asked Clive in her grating voice, "between bein' called 'nigger' and 'nigro'?" It was the next day, and this discussion was taking on its own momentum.

He turned patiently. "'Negro' is a group of people; 'nigger' is someone who steals, who's bad. Not anybody can be called a Negro, but anybody can be called a nigger."

"So if someone says 'Hey, nigro!' or 'Hey, nigger!' there's a difference." She spat out the words as if she were barking orders from across the room.

David turned around. "Would you like someone to say 'Hey, Caucasian!'?"

"Christie!" I couldn't stand it any longer., "It's disrespectful!"

She whirled, her hair on fire. "You don't know anythin' about this! You're a teacher and this is between teenagers!" My face stung as if I'd been slapped.

The fat, shy girl at the back echoed, "This is between teenagers, miss, yer a teacher."

"So what are some other slang words for nigroes?" Christie continued.

Clive squirmed in his seat. "I don't know."

I walked down the aisle to her desk, my heart thumping. "Christie," I said quietly, "you can't talk to me that way."

She grinned. "I don't mean it."

"The next time you do, you'll be kicked out." It had taken me a while to get up the courage. I rolled the words around on my tongue, enjoying their taste.

She raised her face, smooth with practised contrition. I looked into those black eyes, glittering with energy, the high cheekbones, the strong, hawkish nose. I couldn't wait to kick her out!

"Miss, do you think racialism will ever go away?" Clive's voice trembled.

"Well . . . I . . . ."

The bell rang.


Their prejudice was so pervasive, so unashamed. History had shown where that kind of prejudice could lead. I couldn't let it go unchallenged. But what could I do?

The level of prejudice was shocking, I said to Mr. Taggert at lunch that day; were there any guidelines from the board on how to handle it?

An advisory committee on multiculturalism and race relations had recently been formed at the board level, he told me; the Guidance Department had just received its first policy statement.

The cover of the glossy pamphlet showed five cubes tumbling out of a white background decorated with small squiggles that looked, at first sight, like bacteria under a microscope. On the sides of the cubes were photographs. The cube in the foreground displayed the faces of a pretty Chinese teenager, a cute, pony-tailed black girl, and a freckled, red-haired boy; a cube farther back showed an Asian child with no front teeth; relegated to the distant back corner was a blond WASP lady smiling pleasantly, seemingly unperturbed either by the growing ascendancy of foreigners in what was once a white, Protestant Scarborough or by all those swarming bacteria.

Inside was the message from the chairman of the board:

> Scarborough Board of Education trustees are proud of the board's Race Relations, Ethnic Relations, and Multicultural Policy . . . [which] will ensure that learning and work environments within the Scarborough public school system are free of discrimination, and are filled with opportunity for all, regardless of race, creed, colour, heritage, or religion. . . .

Following this initial pronouncement were excerpts from other, better-known policy statements, which, presumably, would provide the direction: Article 26 of the United Nations Universal Declaration of Human Rights, the Canadian Charter of Rights and Freedoms, and the Ontario Human Rights Code.

All these good intentions. But had they ever come off the page and made their way into real life? A recent poll published in the *Toronto Star* revealed that about 30 per cent of a random sampling of Canadians agreed that all races were not equal. Seventy per cent believed that immigrants often bring discrimination on themselves. Three out of four felt that immigrants shouldn't "cling to their old ways." And one in three said that laws guaranteeing equal job opportunities for blacks and other minorities went too far.

But it wasn't the whole world I had to challenge. Not even all of

Scarborough, where roughly one-third of new residents spoke neither English nor French as their first language. It was only my classes.

If these high-sounding intentions couldn't be implemented with just *one* class. . . .


I looked first for help to the board's policy statements as outlined in its pamphlet. One caught my eye: "The board will continue to develop curricular and co-curricular programs that provide opportunities for students to acquire positive attitudes towards racial, cultural, and religious diversity."

What I needed were concrete approaches, lesson plans. How do you go about trying to dismantle a thought pattern as solid as a building? These attitudes had likely been instilled since childhood, the first scooping out of the foundation when the mother squeezed the young child's hand – yes, a subtle, anxious code passing from her skin to his, as, hand in hand, they walked down the sidewalk towards his first black person. The steel girders added when the father disparaged a cab driver's accent, or his son's choice of friend. The rivets driven in by peers – their easy laughter at racist jokes, their system of acceptance for some, rejection for others.

Yes, to make even a chip in the building's brick and mortar I needed something strong. A hammer! Where could I find a lesson as powerful as a hammer?

I called the board. They gave me a list of curriculum materials with names like "Jigsaw Classroom" and "Cinderella Stories from around the World." Nothing yet for the high schools, they said; the committee was still new, the policy only recently formulated.

There was no help here.

But I couldn't let those comments pass. I couldn't be a bystander, my silence complicity, like those who stood at the curb and watched the Jews being herded down the road, to the trains.

And suddenly a name winged across my mind: Anne.

I began to formulate my plan. . . .


"Pakistani," I said loudly to my junior English class. That got their attention. They looked around.

"Where's the Paki?" Kevin called out.

"Get out the roach spray," his friend Bill laughed.

I gulped. "Say anything that comes into your mind." I had already written "PAKISTANI" in large letters at the top of the blackboard.

The comments came, tossed like garbage as I dutifully recorded:

> curry
> roaches
> dirty
> stink
> laundry on their heads
> wear curtains
> Paki-dot
> where do they get their money?
> cow
> too many of them
> don't try to fit in

"Chinese," I soldiered on.

> rude
> eyes
> can't drive
> taking over Agincourt
> *Asian*court
> dirty
> rich
> smell like fish
> eat sick things
> bad breath
> rotten teeth

"Italians," someone called out. It was a game now.

"Oh no!" someone of Italian background moaned.

> pizza
> enjoy food
> big cars

Gino-mobiles
IROC – means Italians Reek Of Cologne
lots of cash
good to roll

"What. . . ." I took another breath to slow my speeding heart. "What about . . . Jews?"

power
rich
penny-pinching
rich
big nose
rich
taking over
rich

But what about my grandmother, who raised five children on her own in a poor, downtown neighbourhood? What about the rooms she let to seven boarders, the sewing she took in? What about my father's bony legs? – rickets, the doctor diagnosed, years later. What about the university education he gave up, though he won a Gold Medal upon completing high school, because he had to help support his mother, his brothers, his sister? So that one day they could have a rich life. Opportunity rich. Worryless rich.

Yes, my father and mother struggled against disadvantage. And gradually they did climb up, up – finally to the big, beautiful house in Forest Hill where I was born.

I wouldn't tell them any of this. Why should they know anything about my background? Why should I expose myself to their ignorance and cruelty? Never let yourself be vulnerable, Colin Beatty had said.

*Never* would I tell them I was Jewish.

I had to compose myself. "Teenagers," I muttered. "What's the stereotype that adults have of teenagers?" I scrawled "TEENAGERS" across the blackboard.

druggies

alcies
know-it-all
sex
trouble-makers
thieves
liars
jailbirds
dirty
stink
weird hair

I leaned against the board, too agitated to remember that the chalk would smear my sweater. Surely the moral of all this would now be apparent.

"And how many teenagers are *really* like that?"

"Most of 'em," Christie said.

"What?"

"Most teenagers are like that. Most of the kids in this class look like that. Most crimes are committed by teenagers. Look at most accidents. They're caused by teenagers."

"If most accidents are caused by teenagers, it doesn't mean most teenagers cause accidents," I snapped. The plan was going awry!

"Most of 'em are like that," she repeated. She sat back in her seat.

I appealed to the class. "Come on, you don't *really* believe that!" I looked up and down the rows, from face to unresponsive face.

The lesson had backfired. It was as if I'd given permission for them to further disrobe their hate, as if the class had been a meeting of neo-Nazis, where we'd shared common ideology, discovered fellow-travellers. Today the kids told jokes; I, unwitting accomplice, was responsible for introducing their object, the new victim, leading him by the trembling hand to this room. To this forest. Naked, he stood on the lip of dug-up earth; across the way, the German soldier paused to light a cigarette, blow into his cold, red hands.

"Hey, miss," Kevin called out. "D'yuh know how yah get a Jew to cross the 401?" (The Jew looked up from the yawning hole, back towards the men, women, children trudging in a long line through the trees.) "Roll a penny."

"Miss." Bill, Kevin's friend, was not to be outdone. "How do yah form the Grand Canyon?" (His lips moved with words no one will ever know: a dry whisper, the moan of wind, rustle of leaves.) "Just bury a penny and watch a Jew dig."

"What did Hitler get for Christmas?" Christie said.

"What?" the chorus complied.

"A GI Jew and an Easy-bake Oven." She looked at me. "She's not laughin'. You know, GI *Jew* instead of GI *Joe*?"

Grandma! You came from the Ukraine, a young girl in thick wool stockings, a young girl in the hull of a crowded boat. You left your family behind. And where are they now?

"I understand," I cried out. "But it's not funny!"

They wouldn't have been able to say that had they felt some identification with Jews, any more than the cop could crack his truncheon down on a head, shoulders, back, without first dissociating himself, masking the demonstrator as Commie, capitalist, traitor, enemy.

What could I do now?

How could I get them to see past these cardboard faces and stick figures they found so easy to mock? How could I get them to see, instead, men, women, children, hunger, satiety, anger, forgiveness, longing, laughter: this planet's shared humanity?

How could I do this hard thing?

■

# 7

# THE JOURNALS

I pointed to the multi-coloured stack of Hilroy notebooks on my desk. "We're going to write journals," I said to my junior English class. "Every Monday, at the beginning of—"

"Journals! They're so boooring," Christie announced. But journals were recommended as a way to get basic-level students to write. Even Colin Beatty had told me to use journals. ("They're not a substitute for the paragraphs, or the sentence structure exercises. You *are* doing those exercises, aren't you? So don't make a big deal out of the journals. It's just fast writing. You don't even have to read them.")

"Every year in English we do dumb-ass journals," Christie continued, "and there's never anythin' to write about." She turned to the person behind her. "Maybe she wants us to write about what we learnt or seen or heard on the weekend."

He snickered. "Don't think we should tell her *that*."

If, at their age, I'd been handed a new pink or green notebook with crisp white pages, I wouldn't have been complaining as they were now. I'd have been glad of the opportunity to articulate my forming self. It was around their age that I did begin to keep a journal. Right after my thirteenth birthday. After I received my birthday present: *The Diary of Anne Frank.*

I looked around. Only David, up at the front, was hunched over, and Clive was writing too. The rest of the class glared – a sit-down strike. Should I try the method that had worked with the creative-writing class, that soothing technique, like hands on skin?

"Write whatever you want, anything you want." I walked up and down the aisles, adding new words: "There will be no mark for this. I won't even read it." The words seemed to relax them. Now even Kevin was writing, even his friend Bill.

But not Christie. "JOURNALS SUCK!" slithered chalkily across the side blackboard.

Now – at last – my chance.

"Out!" I said to Christie. "Out!" I repeated, to her arrogant cheekbones, her surprised eyes.

With a slam of the door, the noxious cloud of dyed-red hair and the grating voice were gone. The air seemed cleaner. Now the rest of the class lowered their heads in earnest. Now *everybody* wrote.

Well, almost everybody. I lifted out a pale green Hilroy, opened the covers, stared at the pristine whiteness. I ran my hand down the cool surface. I picked a pen off the desk, rippled an inky date in the top right-hand corner. What if, once again, I began to keep a journal? What if I wrote down what was happening during this year?

Inside my head, words began to drum: "Attention, ahem, students of my junior English class!" I imagined that they raised their heads, looked interested. Now, silently, I spoke to the absent Christie, to her fat echo at the back, to the pimply Kevin, to his friend – spoke directly into their faces:

"Isn't it great that all of us are writing journals! But wouldn't it be helpful if I could give you a real example, read to you from the pages of a real diary that was kept by a girl of about your age?

"I want to read to you from Anne's diary, Anne's dear diary, that moved me, forever changed me, when I turned thirteen. But I won't. Because if I did, you would hurt me."

Christie was waiting when I unlocked the classroom door. "I'm sorry," she said. "I'm sorry I spoke to you that way." Her eyes seemed softer, her hair paler. "I didn't mean it. I speak to my friends that way. I speak to my mom that way." Maroon lips parted contritely over teeth.

"Well. . . ." I was rather pleased by her penitence. "Okay, I accept your apology. But you still have to do that journal assignment."

JOURNAL DAY (even tho it's tuesday)

Dear Dairy,
    I am going to start this off by saying I hate my mother. We are havin famly problems and I feel she is taking it out on me. No matter what I do she's gust not satified. So this is the last straw she can go fuck-her-self because I have had enough. Not to worry, I cried for an hour, beat my bed with a broom handle and wrote her a nasty letter so I feel better. I'm going to go to guidance and get a social worker and see if that helps.
    I am so tired I could die, acsuly I wish I were died, it would make it easier for me. I hope life gets better soon. I gust can't understand it. I work hard, but get so little done. *I am going nowhere fast and everyone around me is sucseading.*
Christie

Treat the journals as a weekly exercise, Colin Beatty had said, a jog around the page.

It was sitting in front of me. No one around. I peeked.

Yes, I read it. And suddenly, unexpectedly, found the soft, sad underside of Christie's lacquered skin.

I stared into the bottom cupboard, at the pile of notebooks unattended in the corner. And all of a sudden they were pastel hands signalling that they had something to tell.

But I had no *right* to read them! To invade their privacy! To break my promise.

My insubordinate hand reached out, pried open coloured covers. Picked up a pencil.

But what if they had all written so openly? Did I really want to get involved?

"Dear Christie." My script wobbled uncertainly at the bottom of her page. "Other people think *you're* the one going somewhere fast. Too bad your mom gets you so down. You are" – and here I lied – "a terrific girl. Keep in touch, Mrs. Solnicki."

I watched Christie open the journal. Saw her face flush so pink that for a moment hair and lipstick blended with her skin. Saw her turn to the person behind and show him my comment. He looked up at me. It was, yes, a friendly expression!

Christie tugged at my braided belt as I walked by. "How many belts you got, miss?"

"I never counted—"

"You got a walk-in closet?"

"Well, yes."

"What's a walk-in closet?" The boy behind her sounded interested.

"Lookit her shoes!" someone else chimed in. Now everyone was peering at me, appraising my wardrobe. "They're granny shoes! From the hundreds!"

Kevin smirked. "They're pointy. Like witch's shoes."

Christie gave him a dismissive look. "You don't even know what ladies are supposed to look like!" She studied me. "You wear interestin' things. I'm gonna dress like that." Her hair flickered with each shake. "This is the last day you're gonna see me in jeans. I'm not gonna look like a punk. . . . I'm not gonna look like a girl. . . . I'm not gonna look like a teenager. . . . I'm gonna look like a . . . a . . . *person!*"

∎

From the creative writing class:

### MY DREAM GIRL

> I stood there all alone one morning
> loking at myself in the mirror
> I was a confused girl not knowing where I was goin
>    in life
> I've been living on my own ever since I was fifteen
> my place wasn't the greatest, I thought to myself

Why can't I be like those other rich school girls
there always properly dressed
and me showing up in a grubby old swaet shirt
I stand there but now in a trance
thinking I lived in a palace with big lovely plants
the other girls looked up to me
but then the doorbell rang
I relized I was still the girl in
ragged old jeans.

                              Angie

8

■

## WASTED

What was it that Colin Beatty did with his classes, anyway? "Use over-heads," he was always saying. But I found them awkward and imperson-al, helpful only for the occasional illustration.

Sometimes, passing Colin's room, I glanced in through the glass. The overhead projector was always on. The students were copying from the screen. The projector cast a white glow over them, like moonlight.

Today I had an odd thought: was Colin even there? I opened the door a crack. He was sitting at the back of the room, legs propped up on the desk, squinting at a newspaper in the dimness.

Softly I closed the door.

Trust yourself, a voice whispered.

I looked out at the dazed Monday faces. "How was your weekend?" Raucous laughter between Kevin and his friend. The rest of the junior English class looked at them with the miffed expressions of those who are left out of a secret. "Want to share it with us?" I said.

"Friday night we went to the creek – amazing!" Kevin gasped.

"The Creek? What's that, a club?"

"Naw, a creek, you know, a *creek*! Water, yah know, this wide. . . ." He held his arms apart. "And we had two cids from Joe Bailey."

"No names!" his friend Bill warned. "She could be a narc! For sure Pritchett's a narc," he added.

"You think Mr. Pritchett is an agent for the Drug Squad?" I said sceptically.

Around the class heads nodded knowingly.

"A lot of teachers are. And some students, too," Bill said.

I smiled. "How can you tell?"

"They're the only ones that carry books."

"Okay, no names," Kevin continued impatiently. "So we got these cids from Bailey. . . ."

"Cids?"

"Acid. Little purple pills this big" – he held up his fingers – "that give yah a buzz *this* big!" He extended his arms. Everyone laughed. "You can also get blotters."

"Blotters?"

"A few drops of chemical on paper. You suck 'em, or chew 'em, or put 'em in yer eye."

"Doesn't do much for me," Bill said.

"Well, *you*. . . ." He cast a scornful glance. "Jimmy Hendrix useta put a bunch of 'em under his headband, be up on stage and WHAM!" He fell over backwards, out of his desk. The class laughed more, encouraging him. "We had a coupla cases of beer, but beer don't do nothin' for me when I'm on cids."

"Does for me," Bill said.

"Well, *you*. . . ." He shrugged. "So we're over at the tree, smokin' hash. The heater was makin' trails. . . ."

"What does that mean?"

"The end of the cigarette. When you're on cids yuh can see the white lines of light."

"You mean like sparklers?" I had a sudden memory of innocence: Firecracker Day. My brother and I plunging through the blackness of the backyard, our magic brushes painting swirls and lines.

"Yeah. And I'm sittin' there, peakin'. . . ."

Once more my eyebrows rose.

"God, this woman don't know *nothin'*!" He leaned back in his seat and appraised me patronizingly. "It's when yah reach the top o' yer buzz and yah staaaaay on it." His hand drew a long, level line. "And then these two tarts come by to take a leak, cuz when one tart takes a leak they all. . . ."

"Prostitutes!"

"God, yer just like my mother! Tarts, yah know, tarts, girls 'bout fifteen years old. So one of 'em goes over to the edge of the cliff, drops her drawers, leans back, and" – he guffawed loudly – "falls over! She's covered in mud, cryin' her eyes out." He could hardly talk, he was laughing so hard.

Disgust was swilling in my mouth like vinegar. But the small voice warned: don't judge. "How did it end?"

"Stayed till four o'clock, went home, slept all day. *Wasted!*"

"Wasted," I muttered. My curiosity was sated.


How different from my weekends when I was their age, the Saturday ballet class, then drama at the New Play Society. Sunday bike rides through the ravine. At parties all we consumed were chips, pop, and pretzels. When parents came down the rec-room stairs, to smile, to say hello, we unstuck our glued, dancing bodies.

"Remember yesterday, what Kevin and Bill were saying. Do . . . you *all* do drugs on your weekends?"

"We drink beer too," Kevin corrected.

"I don't smoke drugs with teenagers," Christie said scornfully. True to her promise to become a "person," she'd altered her hair colour. Now it was pink. "I smoke with my mother. And my grandmother is great to toke with.

"First time I came home high my mother beat me," she continued, ignoring my startled expression. "She said: 'Don't you dare do 'em on the street, where you don't know what yer gettin'. You do it in the *house.*'"

"My mom tokes," the fat echo at the back said shyly. "When she first found out I was doin' drugs she kicked me out."

I frowned. "Why did she kick you out if she was using drugs herself?"

"You know, miss, she's her baby 'n' all," Kevin explained.

"My step-dad tokes, but my mom don't touch the stuff," said Bill. "'cept she's growin' a good one, this high." He raised his hand three feet off the ground.

"Hmmmmm, home-grown." Kevin smiled.

"Hey, miss, you do drugs?" someone asked.

Every time I asked them about themselves, they turned it on me. I shook my head vigorously.

"You got a daughter, right?" Reluctantly I nodded. "What would yah do if yah found out yer daughter was doin' drugs?"

"She's too young."

"But when she's older?"

My mind flashed to my daughter sleeping in her bed. On the pink-papered walls around her climbed leafy vines in a repeating pattern, like a hedge. To protect her. And my son, his curls tight with energy even as he slept, the rainbow Marimekko cars whizzing up and down his coverlet.

My children teetered on the brink of adolescence, those deep waters dangerous with drugs, bad friends, crime. I had been a stay-at-home mother for years. Done so many things with them. But would that make them strong enough swimmers? There was no guarantee of a safe crossing.

"Well, I certainly wouldn't *supply* her with drugs!" I snapped.

"What about if yer kid smoked? Would yah let her smoke in yer house?"

"Nobody in my house smokes."

"Well, then, for sure yer gonna have her doin' things behind yer back," several voices chorused.

I was determined to change the subject. "Do you *really* want to do drugs with your parents?"

"Debate!" someone yelled. My eyes jumped to the back wall. On the other side of it was my neighbour, Mr. Pritchett.

"It'd be great," the fat echo said wistfully. "It'd be easier between yah. Easier talkin'." All of them nodded.

So was that the message? The family that gets dazed together, stays together?

David hovered at my desk after the bell rang. He'd been doing that the last few days, reluctant to go on to the next class.

"Did you ever do drugs – when you were young? I mean, really?"

I smiled. "You know, drugs weren't around much when I went to high school. By the time I got to university, and drugs were more prevalent, I was less. . . ." I stopped, searching for the right word.

"Vulnerable," he finished.

That was it, the perfect word! I looked at his dark, over-liquid eyes, his frail chest, his mop of brown hair. David was vulnerable.

"Did . . . any of you ever have Mr. Beatty?" I scanned the faces of my creative-writing class.

It felt wrong asking students about a fellow teacher. Nervously, I glanced at the back wall, seeking any crack in the plaster that might accommodate Mr. Pritchett's ear.

"He gave us these papers stapled together with stick men on the cover," said Angie, the girl with the blond streak in her hair. "And overheads. Boring, boring overheads." Sounds of disgust travelled the room.

"Hey, man!" the small, dark-haired boy who sat beside Ray blurted. "Yah treat us as totally stupid, I'm gonna be what yah think I am!"

It was the first time he'd said anything. Was that why the class went suddenly stiff, attentive? Or was it that he'd unexpectedly unearthed their buried credo?

I wondered, as I looked at the solemn, nodding faces, could the converse be true?

Or was it too late for them?

Since that first assignment, when the creative-writing class had reacted violently to my marking the many errors in their essays, I'd limited myself to comments at the end of their poems. But I couldn't keep that up. Without marks there could be no final grade.

But how could you criticize a construction of thought and feeling that was as delicate as a snowflake? A low mark would lean on a poem, squash it.

D and E and F misspelled "deaf"; I would be covering up my ears when what I wanted was to "hear, receive, admit."

Yet, there was this prickly problem.

"Did you get much spelling in school?" I asked the creative-writing class.

"I had it from grade one to six, and I still suck!" someone snarled.

"It's all those hidden letters, like 'h' and 'u'. . . ." Angie pointed to the word "silhouette" I'd corrected on the blackboard.

Ted spoke up again: "I always hated it when teachers correct yer spelling cause if yer writing a story or somethin', and you screw up on a word, it keeps you thinking through the whole story about that word."

It made him self-conscious, apprehensive. How could he ever write freely when he was always watching, worrying about the fatal errors?

Others had pushed on them the drills, the quizzes; at the end of it all they were here, consigned to this school, partly because they couldn't master these skills.

Why batter them with what they couldn't do? But why not challenge them in other ways? Wasn't writing more than the sum of its mechanical parts?

So what should my standard be? Suppose I rewarded effort with a high mark. If the work fulfilled the terms of the assignment in an unusually effective way, I'd give it an A plus. If it was a sincere effort, I'd give it an A. If sloppy, hasty, lacking effort and love, I'd give it a B minus. C meant poor. Failing was reserved for not handing something in. And if I had to deal a mark, I'd colour it green – more nurturing than bloody red.

Was there an absolute Good, an absolute Excellent? I remembered an experiment in which the same university essays were submitted to different professors. The grades for a paper had varied widely. So why should a collegiate norm be relevant to a basic-level school?

What if, in my private lexicon, A stood for "Arbitrary"?


Because of its simple structure, a "list" poem would be easy to introduce to the creative-writing class. But what should they write about?

"Fears!" Angie cried out, as if a demon had suddenly reared before her. But the class made faces. "Angie's suggestion is a good one," I said, glancing at her again – so urgent had been her cry. "After all, everyone has fears. Especially during childhood." When I was young, I added, I believed a wolf waited, curled under my bed. When my parents turned off the lights I lay, arms locked by my sides, to keep them from being bitten.

I could admit that. I wasn't revealing anything important when I told them that. Not like the fear of a life half-lived, potential squandered.

A few were encouraged to confess their own childhood fears. "But what about the present?" I asked. Angie and several others began to write.

"Does spelling count?" an anxious voice queried.

I glanced at the intercom, locked in OFF: no one to hear my blasphemy. "No," I answered. Down went the head. But Ray scowled from his back seat; as usual, he refused to do anything. Directly across from him, in the other corner, Jack's long white fingers lay open and limp. Sometimes he wrote, sometimes he didn't. He leaned forward and listened, or he stared out the window. Often I caught him looking at me; then my eyes would veer away, as if to avoid a dangerous collision. Both Ray and Jack were absent more and more often.

A girl handed in this:

> If all my friends didn't trust me
> bein raped
> if I had an uncured disease like Aids
> Going out by myself
> Bein laughed at
> bein chased by someone vilent
> skin heads
> dieing
> scared of not bein someone when I grow up

I read them out, maintaining the authors' anonymity, watching reactions. They were tremendously interested in what their classmates had to say, but when it came to their own work they covered their faces in an impassive mask, or looked down at the desk, disguising their identity with indifference.

I came to the last one in the pile:

> Being alone in a taxi at night
> Being alone on a dark cold night
> Seeing your mother that you haven't seen in years,
> or seeing your father and remembring
> all the fears.

The words fell softly, like sand, settling into the crevices in the desks where kids had gouged obscenities, covering the floor in a light layer.

The others had been inventories. So how was it possible that some-one, suddenly, from a list had made a poem, something with rhythm, rhyme, even climactic order? Who had taught him that?

Finally someone broke the silence: "My old man, he lived upstairs, but . . . he kept to hisself. He was always drunk. He drank for forty years. I just got to know him when I was fifteen."

The confession had entered suddenly, summoned by the poem. "How come?" I said, taken aback by this image of a father exiled inside his own house. My own father had been so very present.

"He stopped drinkin'."

"What . . . was he like when you got to know him?"

He thought about it. "A really nice guy!"

Silence again.

Another voice: "My sister useta drink. She had two different person-alities. She come home and bust things up. But since she got a baby she completely changed." He smiled.

And now family revelations jostled for space. "My cousin's a drunk. Drives a beer truck."

"My uncle, he useta work on steel beams, you know, real high on buildings. He'd drink at lunch, like really gulp it down. When he drinks in our livin' room he can't hardly stand. But he walked those steel beams!"

"My grandfather useta drink real bad. He beat my dad. One day my dad knocked his head in, and he left for good. My father seen him a few years ago, sleepin' on a park bench."

"It must be . . . terrible . . . to find your father that way."

The boy stared back.

"My father broke my mother's bones!" a girl cried out, her pretty face transfixed. "He said he'd kill my brother and me if she ran away. One day she had her leg in the door, he closed it, broke it in two places!"

"He *did*? Did she get away?"

"My stepfather got after him."

"Then what happened?" The vortex was drawing me in.

"He's gone too."

I looked at her. Long blond hair, blue eyes, turned-up nose. She was as pretty as any fairy-tale princess.

"My dad, he's a janitor at a bar." It was Ted, the small, dark-haired boy who sat across from Ray. He hardly ever spoke; he rarely handed anything in. Yet he was the author of the poem. "Comes home drunk and gets into fights with my stepmother. My brother 'n' me," his voice climbed – "could put him in the hospital sometimes!" His face turned bright red. "Bastard! Asshole!"

I stared at him. Everyone stared at him. He stared at his desk.

I exhaled heavily, suddenly aware that I'd been holding my breath. "Could I read you something?" I opened the desk drawer, took out the collegiate book of poems.

Suspicion returned to their faces: I was changing back into my enemy uniform. So why was I doing it? I had already tried them on another difficult poem, and that had been a failure.

"It's called" – I paused – "'My Papa's Waltz':"

> The whiskey on your breath
> Could make a small boy dizzy;
> But I hung on like death:
> Such waltzing was not easy.
>
> We romped until the pans
> Slid from the kitchen shelf;
> My mother's countenance
> Could not unfrown itself.
>
> The hand that held my wrist
> Was battered on one knuckle;
> At every step you missed
> My right ear scraped a buckle.
>
> You beat time on my head
> With a palm caked hard by dirt,
> Then waltzed me off to bed
> Still clinging to your shirt.

Silence. They stared. They hadn't understood.

Then suddenly Ted cried out: "My old man, he does a waltz every night!"

Ted handed in a second poem the next day:

> **Roll of thunder**
> **hear my cry**
> **by and by**
> **old man comming down the line**
> **whip in hand too beat me down**
> **but I ain't gonna let the bastard turn me around.**

As I put the paper on his desk his eyes fell to the big green A plus. His mouth dropped. "I never got no A plus before in my life!" he crowed. "I ain't never even gotten no A!"

Around him hands reached for the paper.

But Ray, who never did any assignments, snatched it first. He hunched over, then with a curt, surprised nod returned it to the boy he bullied and beat up so often.

■

From the creative writing class:

### STARS IN MY HEAD

> As I lay there in my bed all doped up
> my head feels as if it is a soft marshmellow
> The party was great it was as if
> the whole universe had been recreated with new people
> and new dreams.
> I first arived as sober as clarified water
> but as the night went on we were enjoying the spiked
>     punch
> that reminded me of the old whiskey barell my father
>     use to make.
> I made one promise to myself and to my boyfriend that
>     night

I wouldn't touch the dope.
I started feeling very daring almost like a daredevil
he left my side and I tryed it
the feeling I experianced was like my head was actualy
coming off
right off and flying through the air like a flying sauser
zooming through the star filled sky,
and the next thing I realized was me myself
all alone in my bed, like a helpless invilid.

Angie

9

■

# WHAT ABOUT FELT?

As the others worked on an assignment, Angie came up and slipped a piece of paper onto my desk:

> Coldness and lonelyness
> feelings of being lost.
> Your heart being so warm for love
> Reaching out and not finding him
> So close but so far.
> He's gone and never will be back
> all I have left is specail time to remember
> I love him now and always will.
> Take good care of him,
> Don't let him be hurt
> Let him know that I care
> Huges and kisses from me.
> See you soon
> Your still the best Daddy there is.

She was the most prolific writer in the class. So why had she brought this particular poem to me and laid it on my desk like a gift?

I walked down the aisle. Was it presumptuous to ask questions? But why else had she given it to me?

"Did your father die, Angie?" I said in a low voice. She raised her large brown eyes and nodded.

I hesitated. "How old were you when it happened?"

"Thirteen. Four years ago," she whispered. Head poised, she seemed to be waiting for more.

"How did he die?" She lowered her eyes; her lashes were silky curtains.

"He was killed," she breathed. "I was stayin' at my grandmother's. I woke durin' the night, I just sat up, I knew somethin' was wrong. I called my mom. She said he was asleep, and she didn't want to wake him. Then she came and got me."

"And . . . ?"

"Shot!" erupted like a pistol. Several heads lifted. "In the garage. There's a court case comin'. They don't know who did it. It was a nail gun. It's used in carpentry. They shot him in the head." I stared at her in horror. How could she even form the words? And now her contrasting hair had new meaning: as if the shock of that sudden death had streaked through the darkness like a bolt of lightning, leaving behind its platinum-blond trail.

"The trouble was," she whispered, "we were so close. We did everythin' together. And then he just got cut off." She brushed away a tear that had gathered on her lashes, dribbled a mascara trail down her cheek.

Out of the corner of my eye I saw the kids crowding the door, taking advantage of my distraction. Now, before the bell, they were gone. Somehow, it didn't matter.

I put my hand on the desk's stained surface, near her pale, painted nails. I felt my fingers tugging to reach hers, but I kept them firmly in their place. "Maybe writing about it will help you, Angie."

"I talk to him every night. Every night I write him a poem."


Colin Beatty flew into the English office, his tweed jacket billowing wings behind him.

"Has anyone seen my overhead projector? Has anyone seen my overhead projector? It's disappeared! Those God-damn kids . . . !" He flapped off in another direction.


On my way to class I overheard two black girls at their lockers. One was speaking in singing Jamaican patois – so musical, but to my ears a foreign language. In class the kids from Jamaica spoke a clearer, more comprehensible English that they reserved for us Canadian squares.

The pretty girl with braids, who was in the creative-writing class, was admonishing her friend for her way of speaking: "Don't be so Jamaicanish. You're in Canada now!"

That made me think of another assignment for the creative-writing class. The focus on childhood had helped certain students, like Ted, open up for the first time. What if they did another list poem, this time on childhood memories? When I read aloud the recollections, might that not be a way of breaking down their prejudices? The Canadian-born kids would see the backgrounds of their immigrant classmates, the concrete, intimate details of other lives.

### SWEET CHILDHOOD MEMRIES FROM JAMAICA

I remember pickin the sweet tropical fruits in my
    homeland.
Shoating birds and lizzards was one of my favorite
    pass time.
I also remember lazing in the hot tropical breeze.
I think makin mud pies was alays the best part of your
    childhood memories.
The aroma of supper being cooked on the open fire
    is great.
But now its time to get back to realty. And although
    being a child doen,t last forever The memories will
    last a lifetime or longer.

"Ray. . . ." I warned, when he snickered at the black boy who was staring hard at his desk.

    child hood me
    too much beatens
    hungry all the time
    stay up late
    go to school
    kiss my mom to bed

see granny on the weekend
pee in bed and floor
set bed on fire

"Pee in bed? Wadda loser!" Ray exclaimed. I glared.

the fresh country smell
the sun always shining
the cain field
the mango tree
lots of dogs
the friendly neighbour
being scared to go to school because if your late the
    teacher will beat you infront of everyone.
climing the trees and throwing down things at
    people.
just picking any fruit right off the trees.
always have to make sure my uniform is press.
My mother left me when I was young and my one
    question is when is she coming back to get me?
I always thought my mother was a plane because when
    I ask for her my grandmother would point to an
    arowplane passing by.

"Teacher ever tryta beat me, he's dead!" Ray warned.

"I hope you didn't mind my reading your poem aloud," I said to the pretty black girl with braids, the last to leave the room. Hers had been the final one. Shyly she shook her head.

"When did your mom leave Jamaica?"

"I was only a couple of months," she said softly. "I didn't see her again until I was eleven."

"Who did you stay with?"

"Uncles, aunts, my grandmother, godparents."

She was a sweet, shy girl; well-spoken, too. "Was that sad?"

She nodded, and for a moment her dark eyes drifted.

Gently I probed. "I didn't quite understand that part about the airplane."

She smiled softly. "They would point to an airplane and say she was there. So I always thought an airplane was my mother. I used to jump up and down, waving. I was always trying to flag my mother down."

And I thought, I shouldn't have been afraid to single her out, I should have asked her that question in class. Then, surely even Ray would have been forced to acknowledge the tender child under those tight braids, dark skin!

Nick Sawchuk, the machine-shop teacher, often sat in a certain corner of the staff-room that the tech teachers, mostly men, had turned into a locker room of dirty jokes and noisy laughter. Athletic, broad-shouldered, with a fair, Slavic face, he was the one who usually arrived to break up student fights. He had once played professional hockey out west; perhaps that's why he seemed comfortable wading into a brawl.

Since the junior English class was reading a play about a boy who wanted to become a pro athlete, I invited Nick in to tell them what it was like.

The low, angry mutter from some of the boys when he sauntered through the door surprised me. The girls' reactions were more what I'd expected: Christie opened her purse, took out a small bag, re-painted her purple lips.

Nick leaned against the blackboard, his strong chest straining against the buttons of his checked flannel shirt. He had just begun his talk when Clive turned around and whispered something to Milos. "Hey, you!" Nick bellowed suddenly. "Yeah, you! Little black boy! Shut your bloody mouth!" He rolled the chalk around in his large hand as if to take aim.

Clive flinched as if he'd been slapped. Kevin laughed loudly. David looked to me expectantly. Clive's face wore a tight mask of humiliation and anger.

I was shocked, too.

I should say something.

What could I say to a fellow teacher?

It was the last day of poetry writing for the creative-writing class. I'd taught them many of the simple forms: the list poem, the cinquain, the rhyming couplet. But I felt the culmination of the study should be free verse. It was within that form, or lack of it, that they could be most creative, most themselves.

I read from Ferlinghetti, from e.e. cummings. As usual, they became hostile when I trotted out examples, analysed style. They looked as if they'd been drenched in a downpour.

"Now," I said, enthusiastically, trying to pierce the muffled clouds, "at last you can be *crazy*! *wild*! It's *free* verse!"

But not this free. . . .

> in the dark depths of hell
> from which I had just fallen into
> so I am finally here.
> and to my surprise it was a hell of a party
> I looked around and all I see is
> wall to wall pussy in every form.
> Then everyone of them jumped me
> there was nothing I could do but love
> my eyes turned red and my dick got hard
> but they wouldn't stop until
> my balls were on fire
> they were the size of two apples and
> the same colour to.
> With my lungs almost calapsed
> and my last breath I screamed for help
> but all I could do was scream
> I love it
> Jesus Christ I love it!

■■■

> She was complaining about her legs
> getting tired, she wanted to sit
> on my face, so I let her besides

who's going to turn down some chick
with a great hole. She was hot
I mean hot. You could put a
couple of icecubes in her hole
and they would melt.

■ ■ ■

The old man sits and smokes his pipe
The doctor told him to stop
he said fuck you
smokin's the only thing I got left
except my bag of weed, my gram of oil
my guitar, and this hot marshall
combo that I stole from Steves music
store back 67 years ago.
So fuck you
by the way do you have a wife named
Venus
because I fucked her with my
penus.

■ ■ ■

Sitting in the class room
smoking a joint the teacher
turn around and called
me a runt

who gives a hell I got
my joint she sends me
down to the office
with the joint

Tagirt looks at me and says
your out for a month
I said who gives a damn

Im high as a    kite
    so dont bother
    me
       get outa
           my
              FUCKEN
                  sight! ! !

"The end of poetry." I put my head down on the cool oak of my desk. Out of the corner of my eye I saw the books on the shelves shift, as if readying to tumble down. A weight pressed on my chest, as if I already lay under them.

Colin Beatty read over my shoulder. "I wouldn't even honour those with a comment," he said sourly. "Just return them and say you want something else."

I raised my face from its burial place in my hands. "Should I say they're in bad taste?"

"*Taste?* Do you think they'll understand what you mean by *taste?*"

"Maybe I should say they're inappropriate and unacceptable."

"Jill, they won't understand the words, let alone the ideas!" He sounded exasperated. "I warned you not to overestimate these kids. But you had to go on, as if this were a collegiate, disregarding my advice, abandoning the course outline." He leaned against the shelves and crossed his arms. "Have you taught them sentence structure? Paragraphing? I see no sign in any of your classes of the discipline that comes from using overheads. Mr. Pritchett has stopped knocking on *your* door, but he is knocking on *mine*! How long can I hold off before I go to the principal with a complaint?" He stared down sternly.

I slumped deeper into my chair. Maybe he was right. These kids. Just when you thought you were making progress they turned on you. It's said that wolves can never be truly domesticated – you treat them with kindness, and then one day they face you, ears flattened, fangs bared. . . .

"But maybe they *will* understand." My voice lapsed into depressed silence. It was early November. Ahead of me lay tomorrow, and tomorrow, and tomorrow.

I sighed. "We're about to start play writing. Maybe they'll smarten up."

"*Play writing?*" Colin shook his head like a vexed parent. "Let me remind you one more time." He took *Teaching the Slow Learner in the Secondary School* from the shelf; irritably his fingers snapped the pages.

As Colin preached on, my mind wandered to others. Ted. It was true he'd written one of those vile poems, guffawing all the while to Ray; but he'd written wonderful poems, too! And what about Jack's first work? And the Jamaican girl's? Inside my crushed chest an anger began to stir, not only towards my students, but towards the author of those smug words.

"Learnt . . . seen . . . heard," I muttered. "What about *felt?*"

10

## NO WAY I'M GONNA END UP . . .

This semester my Referral Room duty, one of those extra jobs teachers had to perform, fell first period, once every four days. From a desk near the door I issued a sign-in slip to late students, or received the students who, even this early, had been kicked out of class.

I hated Referral Room. I hated the line-up of kids, and their lying. I hated the reek of marijuana from a student as he told me he had slept in.

My standard question: "Why are you late?" had given rise to the following statistics compiled in my last tour of duty.

> slept in: 31
> late bus: 5
> car malfunction: 3
> basketball malfunction: 1

I had also dutifully transcribed, in the column beside the names of the offenders on the orange sign-in sheet, several miscellaneous responses impossible to categorize:

> 1. "My goldfish had babies."
> 2. "Three flat tires on the subway."
> 3. "I was tryin' to find the guy that raped a friend of mine."
> 4. "My son wouldn't get up."
>    "Your son?! How old is he?"

"Two. He just wouldn't get up for school."

"Do you take him to day-care?"

"Both of 'em. I got twins."

5. "Actually, I was watchin' Phil Donahue, and there was these fat people sayin': 'Hey, it's okay to be fat. . . .'"

6. "Anythin' you want."

"Why?"

"Cuz I'm late every day."

Kevin jauntily approached the desk. His pimply skin breathed the cold of outside air. He unzipped his down jacket. "I guess I'll have to go to English now." He smirked at his friend Bill.

I looked up irritably. "I saw you at eight-forty in the hall. What are you doing signing in now?"

"I . . . ah . . . had to go to the post office."

"Oh?"

"Yeah, you know, sendin' a letter to my aunt."

"Where's the post office?"

"What's the name of the street back around behind?" He waved a vague hand.

Next. He was big, leather-jacketed. His dark hair fell over his eyes. "Why are you late?" I was supposed to give them the feeling that the system was keeping track.

"Doctor's appointment."

"Oh, sure," Kevin interjected from the door, proving that the guilty make the best interrogators.

The boy pulled his hair aside to reveal a bloodied left ear.

"Oooo!" Kevin said, impressed.

"Someone bit my ear," the boy said.

"Someone bit your ear?" I repeated. "Who?"

"I dunno."

"Wouldn't you be able to get a pretty good view of someone who was biting your ear?"

"I was in a fight. Whole buncha guys on top of me. Mind you, I bit back." His smile revealed a chipped front tooth.

"Where did all this happen?"

"A party."

I shook my head. "Sounds like you go to interesting parties."

"You bet! Last week I got a black eye!"


I looked up from my desk in home-room to see Dori in a white rabbit-fur jacket.

"A few years ago I went to a doctor cuz of malnutrition. I was passin' out, vomitin'. . . ." She had this peculiar habit of beginning a conversation as if hours of intimate talk across a smoky table had preceded it. "When I was twelve I was kicked outa the house; useta drink a mickey a day, take drugs. They took a test, couldn't believe the amount of alcohol in my blood!" She laughed.

Was I supposed to laugh, too?

"Then I met Neil. He's the one bought me this fur coat." Neil. I'd seen the boys trail her down the hall like dogs; maybe he was one of them. "He made me stop all that stuff; said he wouldn't have anythin' to do with me otherwise."

"Well, good for him!"

"Yah see, he'd been through the same thing. When he was thirteen he ran through a plate-glass window – he's got scars on his neck and wrist. After that, he decided not to touch the stuff."

I disciplined my dubious thoughts about this boyfriend and nodded more approval.

Her cheeks flushed. "I told him about yah. D'yah think yah'd like to meet him?" She studied me carefully, gauging my response. "Maybe I'll introduce yah to him some time." Back to her seat she flounced, the jacket a pouffe of white above the twitching bum. She was a tough, knife-toting rocker, but the soft fur cuddling her made-up face didn't seem as incongruous to me as it once might have.


"We've done paragraphs on going to school," I said to the junior English class, "and on going from school." ("Simple, straightforward. . . ." I whispered contritely to an imagined Colin Beatty.)

"What about parents?" Christie suggested. "Like, *mothers*." She scowled and tossed back her now green mane.

"My old lady always kicks me out," Kevin's friend Bill said. He raised his tired-eyed face before it toppled back into a slouch of shoulders.

"Why?"

"I dunno. She just gets mad" – he gave a helpless shrug – "for no reason. Cuz she's mad about somethin' else. Gives me two hours to get my stuff together."

"My old man grabs me by the collar and throws me out the door and throws my stuff after." Clive delivered this with a laugh.

"My old lady threw me out once for three and a half weeks!" Kevin announced, to get everyone's attention. Again he intended to dominate the class. "I slept in front of our apartment building."

"Why did she do that?" I asked. After Kevin had stolen the camera, Mr. Taggert had told me a surprising thing: Kevin's mother was a teacher! I stared at Kevin and tried to picture what it would be like to have him as a son. You were middle-class, educated, and the spin of the birthing table brought you a son who'd dropped to the bottom of the school system, who spent weekends on intimate terms with cids and blotters and trails and peaking.

"She never gets mad at me for the big things, like if I get arrested or busted. But, like, if I skip school or come late, she freaks out! She throws things!" His head bobbed excitedly.

I pictured his mother railing at the Fates for bringing her the wrong son.

"Anything in her hand," he continued. "Pots, pans, a knife. Once she threw a jar of jam. I ducked, it hit the wall, then she was mad at *me* cuz it made a big mess!" He chuckled loudly. "She's got pretty good aim for an old bag!"

The class laughed appreciatively.

"So there I was" – he turned around so that everyone could see him – "sleepin' in front of our apartment. The nights were cold and I only had on shorts. One time these two girls came down and slept on the grass."

"Woo, woo!" Clive interjected.

Kevin ignored him. "They weren't kicked out, they just wanted to keep me company, I guess. People were throwin' water bombs at us."

"What did you eat?" I tried to picture this strange scene.

"Nothin'."

"What did you do for money?"

He laughed. "I had lotsa money. Never had so much money as I had then!"

"But where'd you get it?" I insisted. I was trying to see it through the eyes of the mother, the teacher, looking down from her balcony in a Scarborough high-rise to this tiny dot, her son. He'd fallen from a great height.

He grinned secretively. "Just lucky, I guess."

"Where'd he get the money?" I persisted, to his friend.

"Guess he found it," Bill grinned, as others chuckled.

I seemed to be missing the joke.


Somebody had shoved a wad of paper or pencil lead into the keyhole so that I couldn't get my key in. Somebody – I looked suspiciously at the bodies slouched against the lockers – had done it so that I'd cancel the class. I hoped Mr. Taggert wouldn't stroll by, or, worse yet, the principal. What if, in his inside jacket pocket, against his chest, he was keeping warm, incubating like an egg, the Complaint?

"Here, let me try." Kevin pulled a student transit card out of his pocket, bent his knees, and expertly slid the card up and down while his other hand tested the handle. Nothing. "It works for apartments," he said apologetically.

"I'll call the janitor." I was not going to reward vandalism by giving a spare.

"Wait a minute," Kevin persisted. "I'll come in through the window." He disappeared down the hall. At that moment a boy walked by.

"Yo, Randy!" someone leaning against a locker called out.

Randy swaggered over: regulation black-leather jacket, long greasy hair. "I'D RATHER BE HIGH," proclaimed a button on his jacket. Quickly he appraised the situation. "Let an expert do it." He took out a beat-up plastic card, placed it between the door and the wall, coaxed it, concentrated on it. He rocked on his steel toes; the small, silver marijuana leaf that dangled from his earlobe jiggled. At that moment Kevin's grinning face appeared on the other side of the glass. Simultaneously they opened the door.

"Thank you," I said admiringly. "You're a partnership made in heaven!" Everyone grumbled on past except Kevin. He stayed outside in the hall with this new boy. Heads together, they whispered intently.

Where had they learned that skill for opening doors?

Everyone read with interest the piece of yellow paper that Kevin was circulating. Eventually it reached my hands – a court summons for breaking and entering, theft and assault.

Was this paper the punch line of the joke? "What's the breaking and entering for?"

He smirked. "I was down at my friend's apartment – he don't live there no more – and the door was open, so I went in."

"What's the assault?"

"I got drunk, the super came, I assaulted him."

"Same super you were charged with before?" Bill asked.

"Naw, this is the building next door."

"How can you be proud of that shit?" David tossed off on the way back to his seat from the cupboard that housed the journals. Lately I'd noticed a few kids stealthily withdrawing their notebooks, reading my weekly comment, then slipping the book back into its place. On journal days some were writing responses to my observations. The journals were beginning to feel like conversations, letters, a pile of pen-pals.

I shook my head and sighed. I heard it, a far-off echo, the shake of another mother's head, her sigh. "Why do you do it, Kevin?"

His friend Bill looked at me. For a moment his lidded eyes lifted. "Why do you teach?"

"Our clientele are getting younger and younger," the federal parole officer was saying. He was a husky young man with short hair and a moustache talking into a microphone at the front of the assembly. I was standing against the wall. The other teachers were also standing, along the sides and back, visible, lending an air of control. Like prison guards. Nick Sawchuk, arms folded; Mr. Pritchett, eyes darting.

The speaker had started in a friendly enough fashion. But now, after fifteen minutes, something had changed. It was because of the laughter that punctuated his remarks. "Some of you may take the parole system as something of a joke," he said, breaking off from the prepared text after one particularly loud outburst. He pointed a finger at the audience. "Listen, as a parole officer I have absolute control over you. If I think you should go to bed at nine o'clock, I tell you. If I don't like your friends, I tell you. And if you don't do what I say, I can throw you back in jail!" His finger jabbed the air.

Boos. Hisses. Laughter.

Uneasily, my eyes swept the room. For a second they rested on David, sitting alone near the back. He was hunched, his dark head bent intently forward, as if he were repeating the words from his autobiography: "Get control of myself. . . ." Behind him, Mr. Taggert frowned. He'd authorized this assembly, maybe thinking it would persuade the kids to stay away from crime. But the speaker wasn't winning converts.

"Some of you think you're a tough guy, that you've got the world by the tail." The parole officer scanned faces, seeking offenders. "Well, just try going to prison. First thing when you come in you're just a chicken – a kid with a cute bum!" He waited for the hoots to die down. "Let's say you're a big wheel here. There, you're at the bottom of the totem pole. You're going to be tested. If you stand up for your rights, you'll be beaten up; if you don't, you'll be pushed around. Then there's the psychological terror: you won't know what the guy next to you is in for, and there's maybe three, four in a cell."

Someone sitting near me put up his hand. "I been in East Metro," he said. His hair was shiny clean, his parka powder blue. "It's not as bad as all that." With all the unkempt kids in the school, was this well-dressed one the criminal?

"What floor were you on?" the parole officer said. "First-time offenders are put in the better section."

"Yeah?" the boy persisted. "Well, I been there three times. And I met a guy in there for Murder One, and he was the nicest guy you'd wanna meet!" Now I noticed Kevin beside him. If you couldn't tell a criminal by his appearance, maybe you could by his friends.

The parole officer stared. "I guess you must like it there. I guess I'll be seeing you there," he said heavily. He looked away. "When I walk into a jail now, it looks like a high school. We expect the jail population to triple in the next few years, and it'll be with kids your age. It's pretty disheartening." His voice sank.

I stood at the door as the cafetorium emptied. "What did you think of it?" I asked Kevin as he passed. I reached out, rested my hand on his arm.

His eyes were redder than usual. "No way I'm gonna end up in there!"

"I was in East Metro over the weekend!" the animated, bright-eyed Kevin announced to his admirers. He waved a piece of pink paper. From yellow to pink – was that the progression? "Got to watch TV all day. Really soft! One of the guys in my cell was in for murder – someone raped his sister!" He looked around proudly.

David frowned. "I'd go after someone with a forty-four, he did that to my sister."

"I'd give her to him!" Bill retorted.

"Kevin, were you scared?" I asked quietly.

"Naw, they were nice guys. The cops beat me with their billy sticks, though. I got a mark here." He raised his Iron Maiden T-shirt. Everyone peered at his thin, hairless midsection. "They go 'poom!'" He pushed the invisible butt against his chest. "But I only have one mark, so I can't charge 'em." Everyone looked impressed.

"Me!" Bill interjected. "They used two fists with this telephone book in between. Wham!" No one took any notice.

"They found three thousand dollars' worth," Kevin said. "Nice VCR, stereo equipment, diamond rings. They were tryin' to find out where the rest of the four thousand is."

I leaned against the desk.

"I'll take one o' them rings!" Christie said. "You got any emeralds? – it's my colour." She touched her green hair.

"What did your mother say?" I said quietly.

He shrugged. "Just took me for a pizza when I got outa the cop shop, asked me what it was like in prison. Asked me where I did it. Didn't ask why, though; they know why. It's cuz they never give me no allowance."

The pink piece of paper had finally come to me. It was a list of bail conditions:

1. One thousand dollars' bail for Breaking & Entering three times.

2. A curfew from 5:00 p.m. to 8:00 a.m.
3. No loitering within 100 metres of the Riviera Court
   Townhouse Complex.
4. No skipping school.

I looked up. "Kevin, do you feel this will keep you from doing these things again?"

"Yeah! Cuz I really messed up this term, right? Next term's gonna be good, right? I'm gonna come every day, right? I'm gonna go to every class, right?" The bravado had dropped like a mask.

"You never gonna B and E again?" Bill said plaintively.

"Nope!" he exclaimed. "At least, well, not for a while."

"Wanna skip class tomorrow?"

Kevin grinned. "Sure!"

The vice-principal's voice boomed over the PA: "May I have your attention, please! Three computers disappeared from the keyboard class over the weekend. Anyone with information regarding this incident should see Mr. Taggert as soon as possible in the front office!"

## 11

■

## FIELD TRIP

When I was a child my parents often took me to the museum, and even now, in my mind, it remained a place of mystery. Though it had been remodelled, I still pictured the scratched yellow hardwood floors, the shafts of dusty light, the looming dinosaurs and nightmare mummies. My students were sharing much of their lives with me. Why shouldn't I share a bit of mine with them? A harmless bit.

I spoke to my home-room class about a field trip. They were pleased at the prospect of missing school.

In the front foyer, before announcements, I handed out a sheet: "The Dos and Don'ts of School Excursions." It boiled down to one message: Don't Embarrass Your School. That established, we headed out the front door into the drab day. Everybody was in high spirits, although the bushy pines were the only sign of green in a grey, blurred, November landscape.

We waited in a cluster for the traffic to ease up before we crossed Kingston Road, our breath rising in small, smoking clouds.

Suddenly Gus darted ahead and lay down, spread-eagled, in the middle of the two westbound lanes. I stared at the horizontal body wrapped in its wine-coloured ski-jacket shroud. Then I found my voice.

"Gus!" I screamed. It was a wide, busy road. A transport truck was bearing down, honking its loud horn.

He got up and ambled back to the curb.

"Why did you do that!" I panted.

"Jamie bet me three dollars."

The bus was coming. We ran across and clambered aboard. John looked out the window. "Ain't that Kevin Smythe and Randy Edwards?" He banged loudly on the glass. I swung around. Sure enough, the two boys were striding down the sidewalk, their heads bobbing in animated talk. How nice that my introduction had apparently led to friendship. But what schemes were these two cooking up? "Hey, you're skippin' school!" John shouted. He banged some more. I banged too: Kevin was already breaking one of the conditions of bail. Two seats ahead an old woman turned, tight-lipped, and frowned at me. The bus stopped at a corner. "I know her," Dori said, sighting a girl waiting to cross. "What a slut!"

"Where? Where?" Leroy half stood and pressed his mouth against the opening in the window. "Hey, honey, spread your legs!"

More people glared. An old man sighed.

"Shut up, can't you see you're botherin' people?" Dori said, wrinkling her turned-up nose. At least someone could control them.

On the subway platform I counted my flock like an anxious shepherd. Suddenly Leroy hurtled by and jumped down onto the tracks.

"My God! Leroy!" People turned, horrified. The train would come at any moment; I could hear its far-off thunder. "Leroy!"

He lifted his long legs and hoisted himself back onto the platform. "They said that rail over there would kill yah. I said it wouldn't." At that moment the train roared into the station and shrieked to a stop. I had a flash of Leroy under its long, low-slung, silver body.

"You could have been killed, Leroy!" A wide grin lit up his face.

The subway dumped us at the corner of Yonge and Bloor streets. This was my territory, as the malls were theirs, this narrow grid of expensive restaurants and fashionable shops – Avenue Road, Bloor Street, Yorkville, Cumberland – where I had spent the leisure hours, the restless days that added up to years. Birks winked its jewelled eyes from across the street. The mannequins in Holt Renfrew's windows looked down on us haughtily as we passed. The uniformed doorman studied us, his brow knotted. I looked away self-consciously. It was strange to be back here, in my old haunt, in different company.

A slim man in a well-cut navy suit hurried past, his leather attaché case swinging. "Fuckin' freaks here!" Gus grimaced.

A woman in a dark mink swept by, the corner of her coat brushing

Jamie's leg. "Anything can happen to yah here!" he whispered, recoiling. We watched her disappear into Holt's glittering gullet.

At the southwest corner of Avenue Road and Bloor the museum waited, an old friend. The façade was soft grey in the subdued morning light. It was reassuring that the stone lions still sat on each side of the steps, their heads resting on their paws, as if nothing had changed, as if, in a museum's calendar, in the time span of civilizations – of Mesopotamia or Egypt – a few lost years were nothing.

At the side door, the entrance for school groups, we were met by a tall, swarthy man of upright bearing, his photograph clipped to the lapel of his tweed jacket. I thought he might be East Indian.

"You our guide?" Gus said.

"I am not a guide," he said, standing even straighter, "I am a teacher." Each word terminated precisely as if it had been snipped off. His black eyes swept the large buttons on the kids' jackets: "IF I WANTED TO HEAR AN ASSHOLE I'D FART"; "DON'T KISS ME STUPID, FUCK ME SILLY"; "IF YOU'RE CANADIAN SHOW ME YOUR BEAVER"; "IF I WANTED YOUR LIP I'D UNZIP MY FLY"; "AN 11 IS A 10 THAT SWALLOWS." The small, discreet ROM buttons he handed out looked out of place beside them. "Take off your jackets," he said tightly. He pulled a coat rack out from the wall.

"Why?" everyone said in unison. They looked shocked.

"Because this is a class. You don't wear your jackets in school, and you don't wear them here."

"I ain't fuckin' takin' off my jacket!" John growled. He'd worn black-leather pants today to match his leather jacket and black cut-off T-shirt. He'd dressed up, to acknowledge the specialness of this day.

"Excuse me." I beckoned the teacher aside. He didn't know these kids, that they never took off their jackets, never. "These are basic-level kids. You know, from one of the special schools. Could you please be, well, *basic* with them?"

His face froze. Then a light came into his dark eyes. He went over to John. "You wouldn't want to hide that, would you?" he said, pointing to John's nail-studded leather belt. "No one can see it with your jacket on." Warily John looked back.

"John," I said quietly, "you can keep your jacket on if you want."

"He said to take it off, so I'm gonna take it off!" His face looked stricken, as if he might cry. He slipped out of two sets of sleeves. His black

T-shirt hugged his ribs. His arms were white and thin. He was scrawnier than I'd ever imagined. Gus took off the torn wine ski jacket. I'd always assumed he was chubby, but he too was narrow-chested. Self-consciously they hugged their bodies, as if they were naked. I looked away, humiliated for them.

The teacher led us down the stairs, along a corridor lit with fluorescent ceiling lights, and into a classroom. On the tables sat a row of skulls like expectant, bald hosts. Beside them were stacks of papers. Our lesson was to be on evolution – at my request. If they came to see the products of civilizations, surely they ought to know how it all began.

"Study the skulls on your table, then fill this in," the teacher instructed, indicating the papers. I picked one up. It was a comparison chart of primates. My eyes stumbled across the columns, past "sagittal crest" and "foramen magnum," over the daunting "Australopithecus boisei," around "Homo sapiens neanderthalensis."

The students stared at their charts. The teacher stared at me. I stared at him. He collected the charts.

He picked up a skull and cleared his throat. "This is a copy of Homo habilis. He lived two million years ago. We developed from him." In his other hand he held up a chimpanzee skull. "See the similarities? Our cousins."

Dori broke the stunned silence. "That's not true," she muttered, from my table. "That's not true," she repeated, louder.

The teacher picked up another skull. Perhaps he hadn't heard her. "Excuse me," I said hesitantly, "but Dori here doesn't believe you." I was glad I wasn't in his place.

"Well," he said, calmly, pleasantly, "we *do* have the evidence. On the other hand, we can't dispute the Bible. One is scientific fact, the other psychological fact." Dori glared at him as if, within those words, an insult lurked. He returned to a drawing of Homo habilis, pointing out the sloping forehead, the hair covering the body, the protruding jaw. He explained how certain physical features were developed, or lost, as part of an adaptation to environment.

"Wait a minute," Gus interrupted. "Yah mean, if I lived for three years in the cold, I'd grow hair all over my body?"

The teacher stared at Gus. He seemed to be making a decision. "Well . . . sort of." He located a piece of lint on his sleeve, carefully picked it off, then turned to another skull. "Does this look familiar? This is Homo sapiens. That's the family we're in."

"Hey, there's no homos in my family!" Leroy interjected. "He's callin' us faggots!"

"That's homo*sexual*." The teacher blinked three times in rapid succession.

"Did them guys eat dinosaurs?" Jamie asked.

"Dinosaurs lived long before people existed."

"Before BC?" Jamie exclaimed. "Before Adam 'n' Eve?"

"There was a lot that lived before people came along." The teacher forced a smile. "The first life was micro-organisms."

"Micro-orgasms?" Leroy said, perking up.

"Well, that's about it for evolution. . . ." Down went the picture, back went the skulls to their case, where they would sit hollow-eyed, longing for their lost bodies. "We'll go to the galleries now."


The first gallery was Africa. We peered through glass into a minute of jungle day. A green tangle of vines, huge butterflies and, crawling up the river bank, a crocodile.

"I'll tell you a gross story about the crocodile," the teacher said, trying to get basic. "One day they discovered termites inside this crocodile; it was being eaten from the inside out!"

"Gross?" Leroy said. "I'll tell yah gross. Gross is yer grandmother bendin' down to kiss yah goodnight and slippin' yah the tongue."


A mummy lay in its opened sarcophagus, its black hair patchy, skin parchment, fingers nibbled to different lengths. Perhaps it was the mummy from my childhood, its teeth still bared in the same grin I remembered, as if it were enjoying some joke about mortality.

"Gross me out!"

"Gross me to the max!"

"Arghhh!" Someone made the sound of vomiting. But John's attention was caught by a dish in the next case. "Is that real gold?" he asked, wide-eyed.

"Yes, it's gold leaf," the teacher said.

"That's priceless, right?" John continued excitedly. "Like, is there a price for that?"

"No," the teacher said.

He squeaked at a vase. "Is there a price for this?"

"It is priceless," the teacher said.

"How much would it take to buy that?" He pointed to a silver coffee urn.

"Oh, about fifty thousand dollars."

Leroy's face grew thoughtful. "What time you close this place?"


The Chinese gallery sported a large, stone Buddha-like statue, its palm raised. "Hey, a chink!" Leroy announced.

"Leroy . . . ," I warned. I had made a resolution: whether or not I could ever pierce their thick prejudices, I wasn't going to let their slurs pass by. They should know that at least one person did not go along; not everyone in the crowd picked up a stone.

"That's not a Chinese person," the teacher said, choosing each word carefully. "That's the monk Luohan. You know, the Chinese had a civilization long before us. They had writing, and—"

"Yeah, but who can read it?"

"Did you know that one out of five people in the world is Chinese? Chinese is the most commonly spoken of all languages." He had the kindly, careful tone of someone who believes that the simple facts will clear up this misunderstanding called prejudice. Hadn't I thought that too?

"I know who doesn't know nothin' about birth control," John chortled. "The chinks!"


Our last destination was the dinosaurs. We walked in single file down a trail dimly illumined by sunlight filtering through the tangled forest ceiling. On each side hulked huge skeletons – the gentle diplodocus bending to nibble vines, the brontosaurus towering in the ferns. "These ain't real, are they?" Jamie whispered.

"I'm not sure," I whispered back.

On our way to the main rotunda, four middle-aged women passed us going the other way. They were attractive, slim, expensively clothed, their blouses set off by pearls and amber beads. I recognized them. The volunteers. Instantly I knew where they lived, whom they'd married, where they holidayed, that they toiled for the ballet, the opera, the art gallery, or their favourite disease. I could tell by their hushed, reverential tones that they thought this museum was a temple where they did holy deeds. I could tell by the way they looked at my students, the way they cringed to avoid touching them as they passed on the stairs. For a moment I felt embarrassed to be in such company, to be getting my hands dirty in some foreign, faraway, low-class part of town.

Dori turned around and looked after them. Her pouty lips curled disdainfully. "Snobby bitches!"

The echo of those words bounced off a distant wall in a dim corridor, my first day at school. Two months ago. A long time.


"Maybe we could write a report about our field trip for the school newsletter?" I stood in front of the blackboard, chalk poised.

"We saw live mummies!" Gus began.

"Some Paki made us take our jackets off."

"Paki*stani* is the prop—"

"He told us we're related to gorillas!"

"We wear jeans and jackets so we don't need to grow fur no more."

"The front hall is made of gold!"

"Everythin' is priceless! Like there's no price for it!"

"I went in one of them movie porno places on Yonge Street afterwards."

"I went to the Zanzibar. Chicks dancin' on the tables! All nuuude!"

"I know where Leroy went. He went to the Eaton Centre—"

"Shut yer mouth," Leroy growled, "or I'll ram my fist down yer throat!"

"Miss Solnicki and me went to Holt . . . Holt. . . . This real expensive store. You should see how much a skirt costs there! I saw the exact same one on Yonge Street and. . . ."

"So." I coughed. "How would you sum up our field trip?"

"I got somethin' good out of it, miss." Gus nodded encouragingly.

Could I be held responsible for their activities after we'd parted? And why was Dori advertising our little side-trip? "What's that, Gus?" I looked towards him hopefully.

Gravely he folded his hands on the desk. "I put a down payment on a waterpipe."

12

SCENES FROM . . .

SCENE: *The creative-writing class at Sir Mackenzie Bowell Secondary School.*

*The* CURTAIN *rises on twenty kids sitting in desks, on desks, or lounging on the radiator between the windows,* STAGE RIGHT. *The room is dim. A* TV *flashes:* "Don't Hit Me, Mommy!" *The credits roll.*

*The teacher turns on the lights, and blinks. She peers at the kids as if for a moment she's surprised to see them.*

*Jack, a red-haired boy at the back, stares out the window. Ray, a tall boy in the other back corner, scratches his crotch. The Good News Bible Girl appears to be mouthing words to herself.*

TEACHER: Well. That was an interesting film on child-abuse, wasn't it?

RAY: Faggoty! Gay!

TEACHER *(clears throat nervously)*: Ray, those are put-down words. In any event, the correct meaning of "gay" is "*happy.*"

RAY *(sneering)*: So?

TEACHER: Our reason for watching this drama was to get an idea of how to write scenes. We're going to be doing some . . . ah . . . play writing.

SHY BOY AT BACK *(softly)*: My cousin's a faggot.

*(Class swivels around as one in their seats.)*

SHY BOY AT BACK *(his face colouring)*: His brother saw him at the bus station, broke his nose.

TEACHER: Because he's homosexual?! The proper term, you know, is . . . *(she says word slowly, deliberately)* . . . hom-o-sex-ual.

SHY BOY AT BACK: No. Cuz he left home without tellin' his mother.

RAY *(stretching legs under desk)*: If I found out my kid was a faggot I'd kick the crap outa him every night!

TEACHER *(looking pained)*: Do you *really* think that would change him?

RAY *(rubbing the tattoo on the back of his hand)*: Make him think twice about it!

TEACHER: Could we please get back to. . . .

*(She hears a rhythmic click from the back corner, sees Jack opening and closing a switchblade, as if in a trance.)*

Jack . . . please. Jack!

*(He suddenly snaps out of it, puts knife away.)*

RAY *(to teacher, while sinking lower into his seat)*: What'd yah do if yah found out *yer* kids was havin' incest?

TEACHER *(blinking hard)*: Let's concentrate on play writing. . . .

SHY BOY AT BACK: My cousins're havin' incest.

*(Class swivels around as one in their seats.)*

TEACHER: How do you know?

SHY BOY AT BACK: Everyone knows. They hold hands. They sleep together.

RAY *(snickering)*: Strange family you got.

SHY BOY AT BACK *(blushing)*: And my grandparents . . . no, never mind.

RAY: Come on!

SHY BOY AT BACK: They're cousins or somethin'.

ANGIE: That mother in the show shouldn't have beat her kid like that. I guess she couldn't cope no more.

*(The teacher nods. Her expression reveals familiarity with the afore-mentioned state.)*

GOOD NEWS BIBLE GIRL: People have different things that break 'em. . . .

*(A Bible lies on her desk. Title: Good News Bible. Her fingers tap the blue cover of book.)*

GIRL AT BACK: My mother, when she divorced, she brought up five kids alone. She never hit us—

TEACHER *(interrupting, wistful)*: She was strong.

GIRL AT BACK: . . . unless we were bad.

GOOD NEWS BIBLE GIRL: I know a girl *(tap, tap, tap)* I won't say who *(tap, tap, tap)* her mom useta wake her up when she got home from work *(tap, tap, tap)* and beat her.

*(Class swivels around as one in their seats.)*

GOOD NEWS BIBLE GIRL: She useta sleep with a pillow over her head for protection. It's better now, though *(tap, tap, tap)*. Her grandmother moved in *(tap, tap, tap)*. Now her mother beats her grandmother instead.

TEACHER: My God! Why doesn't your friend leave?

GOOD NEWS BIBLE GIRL: *(Her hand suddenly stops.)* Where will she go?

*(The students in the creative-writing class all turn to stare at The Good News Bible Girl's stricken face.)*

*(The lights dim, except for a* SPOT *that comes up on her body, then shrinks to hold on her face.)*
*(The* SPOT *dims, then goes out.)*
*(*CURTAIN*)*

I'd recorded that class into my journal to practise scene writing. If I could do it, I could teach it. But *why?*

Prose, with its structure and syntax, was difficult for them to write. But their anecdotes were full of realistic dialogue and dramatic conflict. If they'd failed to partake with enthusiasm and proficiency in humanity's written legacy, they certainly shared the oral tradition. Now, if they could only capture that vivid story-telling on paper. . . .

> Ted: Hi mom weres the old man
> mom: he's in a pissed off mode
> Ted: what is new. O shit here he comes O no he is heading
>     for my room
> mom: Ted did you clean it up this morning

Ted: no
old man: Ted come over hear now
Ted: Shits going to hit the fan
old man: move it or Ill smash you out punk
Ted: go for it asshole
old man: ok its your face

(*The old man tries to punch Ted he only got one shot when Ted went ape shit he beat the snot out of the old fart. . . .*)

■■■

(*. . . Girl walks in door.*)

girl: Your drinking, arn't you
mother: yes, but just for today I'll stop tomorrow
girl: Bullshit that's what you say every time, Why did you have to start drinking again you were doing so well three months gone down the drain.
mother: Kim don't yell at me I got a head ace.
girl: Every time I come over you are drinking or are drunk I'm sick of it, the only time you get up is to get another drink or go to the bathroom and you never eat any thing, thats not good for your health.
mother: I'm hungry how about going out and get us something to eat, I'll treat.
girl: Don't try that again you think by buying me something I'll stop bugging you and beside you can't afford it especaily after buying a twenty dollar bottle of vodka. . . .

■■■

(*. . . In the cafeteria*)

Lorraine: I have something to tell you guys
Fay: Spill your guts
Lorraine: I am pregnant!

Althea: So is my great grandfather
Lorraine: Im serious.
    (*She pull her top up halfway and show us her tommy*)
Fay: How many months?
Lorraine: Three
Althea: Why didn't you tell us?
Lorraine: I didn't know how to.
Sherene: Do your parents know?
Lorraine: Yes
Althea: Did your mother flip
Lorraine: At first but it's o.k. now she's excited.
    We sat up till one oclock picking names.
Althea: So you going to keep the baby?
Lorraine: Of course
Althea: Did you tell Winston you are pregnant?
Lorraine: Yes I did but he said he is sterile
Althea: In other words the slime bag doesn't
    want it. . . .

I held up a fistful of papers covered in green marker. "I'm so happy, Colin! The creative-writing class took the play writing seriously! They wrote really honest scenes! With good dialogue, and—" I stopped. Colin's expression was not encouraging. "Anyway," I ended quickly, "they've shown their maturity here, so I'm going to let them work in groups on the next set."

He stared sceptically across the rim of his coffee cup.

### SCENE 4

(*scene: Bell rings. Students walk into the classroom.*)

Teacher: Get the fuck in here, you slimy runts!
    (*The teacher's wearing this sexy outfit, white see-through
    T-shirt, no bra, and these tight, white jeans.*)

    (*The students sit. All the boys stare at her, but Ted sat
    and drooled, the guy made a pig of himself.*)

Ted: (*Sucking back his saliva*) Hey Ray, I never thought
   I would see a sub like that.
Ray: Dam right. Good thing Solhickeys away today.
Teacher: Would someone please help me with atendance?
Ted, Ray, Cliff: I will!
Ray: I will, sexy . . . I mean, miss.
Teacher: Miss Nude World. I won last year so call me
   by that name. And what's your name?
Ray: My name is Ray, Miss Nude World.
Teacher: Okay, Ray, come up here and help me.
Ray: With plesure, miss.
Ted: Ray, you jerk, how come you get the good ones and
   I get the bad ones?
Teacher: Shut up, feminen boy.

(*After Ray finishes taking atendance the teacher french
necks with him.*)

Ray: Miss, I . . . I . . . got to . . . go to the can! This is too
   much for me to handle!

(*Just as Ray is leaving Mark and Rick walk in. There eyes
allmost fall out.*)

Rick: Look at those niples, Mark!
Mark: I'm looking!
Rick: I wonder what they taste like?
Mark: Bet there the best pear you ever tasted.
Rick: (*walks over to teacher and lifts up her skirt.*) Miss, do
   you mind if I take some samples?
Teacher: No, go ahead, I'd love you to, but save some for
   the cute one that walked in with you.

(*Ray walks in the door, looking quite releeved, with a
smile on his face.*)

Mark: Hey Ray, what's happening?

Ray: That sub has the hots for me, man!

Mark: That's funny, it looks like the teacher is all out for Rick.

Ray: WHAT! (*he looks over at teacher and Rick*) You son of a bitch, Rick, I'm going to kill you!

Teacher: Calm down Ray, everyone's going to get some.

Ray: OH WOW! OH WOW!

■ ■ ■

SCENE 5

*Characters*:  Ray
Ted
Rick
Mark
Miss Solhickey
Milos, a geek Greek in miss Solhickeys other class.

(*Mark and Ted are in the underground parking lot in their new, hot station wagon.*)

Mark: Pass the dube, Saunders, don't hog it all.

Ted: Why don't you just fuck right off, jerk?

Mark: What time is it?

Ted: I don't no, stupid.

Mark: Well look at your god dam watch!

Ted: okay you puke, it's 12:03.

Mark: SHIT! WE WERE SUPPOSED TO MEET RICK AND RAY AT THE BACK!

Ted: Oh yeah I forgot, sorry man.

Mark: It figuers. Yesterdays sub was right, you are a feminen boy.

(*In the mean time, Rick and Ray are at the bank. They blow up the vault and get the money.*)
(*The car pulls up. Rick and Ray hop in.*)

Ray: What took you assholes so long?
Ted: It's a long story.
Ray: Who's that! Give me the binoculars!
?: It's miss Solhickey.
Ray, Rick, Ted, Mark: WHO THE HELL SAID THAT?
?: I did. (*Milos pops up from the back of the car.*)
All together: How the hell did you get in here, funky?
Milos: I snuck up on yuse guys.
Ray: (*To Rick*) I hate gay faggots!
Mark: Miss Solhickeys phoning the police!
Ray: Not any more.
    (*He grabs the shotgun, takes aim, and pulls the
    trigger. Miss Solhickey screems peercingly as bullets
    seer her chest.*)
Ray: Get the rope, Ted.
Milos: Why?
Ray, Rick, Ted, Mark: Shut up homo.
    (*They tie Milos up. Because he told on them they kick shit
    out of him.*)

    (*Sudenly they hear sirens.*)

Ray: Shit, not again!

    (*Rick crawls to the back of car and picks up his* M-60.
    *Soon as the cops pull in he lets the bullets fly.*)

Ray: Good. Now let's get out of here.
Milos: (*As they take off in the car*) But don't leave me here,
    boys!
All four of them: Bun-splitters don't deserve to live!
    (*They shoot him too.*)

Colin Beatty had said: "Never let yourself be vulnerable." Believing in these kids, wasn't that a kind of vulnerability? They smelled it, they saw my hand reaching out. To be bitten.

I'd watched Ray, and I'd thought: maybe he's coming around – even as he was destroying my trust, undermining my work, and finally, killing me off in that vulgar, violent fantasy.

But why? Did he and the others have so much self-loathing that they couldn't bear to be liked? Were they so bonded to failure that any success had to be undone?

I sniffled into the plays. But my hurt would stay hidden, the spring behind the eyes a secret. I'd be more careful next time. They wouldn't catch me being vulnerable again!

Colin leaned against the bookshelves, his smugness barely masked. His hand rested on that book he was always reading to me; his fingers drummed an impatient rhythm on its cover: overheads, overheads.

"By the way, last week Hugh Pritchett found one of those free-verse abominations your students wrote; your comments . . ." – he paused significantly – "your *green* comments, were all over it! Want to know what he said? 'Did you know this is going on in *your* department?' Let's just hope it doesn't get passed on to the principal." He speared me with a long, sharp look.

"And while we're on the subject, you'd better not put those poems and plays into that book you're writing."

"What book?"

"The one you're always jotting things into."

"Colin, I'm not writing a book! That's a journal I'm keeping, along with the kids." I gave a weary laugh. "Listen, I could barely get myself out of the house and back to work after ten years. *Me* write a *book*?"

13

■

# BABIES

The police cruiser pulled out of the shopping plaza on the corner of Ellesmere and Morningside Avenue, swung alongside my car, then signalled for me to pull over. Now it was my mind that was speeding.

"Your licence, please," he requested politely. The black book was already open.

I turned off the ignition. "There's a reason why I'm in such a hurry," I stammered. "You see, I'm a teacher. Usually I'm at school early to open my home-room class, but this morning. . . ." I stopped, reluctant to confess my dismay when the alarm clock punched me out of sleep, my growing tendency to burrow back under the welcoming pillow. No other reasons sprang into my head.

He looked up from his book. "School? What school?"

"Sir Mackenzie Bowell. I'm a teacher there."

"You teach at *Bowell?*"

"Yes."

He closed the black book and shook his head. "Anyone who teaches at that school deserves sympathy, not a ticket!"

I was on hall duty when I spotted the girl standing at the secretary's desk in the Guidance office, a baby in the small carriage beside her. Curious, I went in. The baby studied me. I smiled and it smiled back.

"How old is it?" I asked.

"Three months," the girl muttered. She was hefty, with a black T-shirt.

Blond fuzz, big blue eyes, a dimpled chin. "Cute baby!" I exclaimed. The mother made a face. "He cries all the time. Spoiled rotten."

Spoiled meant consciousness, manipulation. How could a three-month-old baby be spoiled? I felt a stab of anxiety for it. We exchanged looks. In my head I heard the words: "But what am I?/An infant crying in the night;/An infant crying for the light;/And with no language but a cry."

"But babies cry," I said. "My son cried during his entire first year. He was colicky. He had indigestion. Three-month-old babies have a very sensitive digestive system," I added urgently.

"I took him to the doctor. She said he wanted to be held."

I nodded vigorously. "If I were three months old, I would want to be held!" Blankly she looked back.

"I had a party, he was up all night. He's a brat." She gave the carriage a shove.

I followed her out into the hall. Two girls wandering by with hall passes stopped.

"Can I hold him?" one of the girls said. "I never get to hold him."

"Yah never phone me," the mother retorted, "so yah can't hold him."

The girl's gaze fell wistfully to the baby before she and her friend wandered off.

The baby looked from my face to its mother's, cooing. It wanted to be talked to. I hoped the mother did that, talked, sang, read to her baby, let it grow up to be the bright child it looked as if it wanted to be.

"I got another kid," the mother said, and ran her hand through her pile of unkempt brown hair.

"Oh." My spirits sank further. "How old?"

"Four."

"Who's looking after it?"

"Its father. He's got no job, so at least he's doin' somethin'," she added bitterly.

The glass doors opened, and the girls with the hall passes wandered back the other way. Again they stopped. "Please can't I hold him?" the same girl pleaded.

"Any time you hold him, he shits. You got a shitty side to your personality!" the baby's mother said. She looked pleased with this new tool of retaliation.

I watched her go out the front door. It was a lovely baby, but we'd exchanged a message through our eyes. That its mother, or its jobless father, would neglect it. Maybe abuse it. But what could it do? What could I do? You couldn't force girls to give their babies up into the mature, loving hands of lonely, childless couples.

Out of his office came the head of Guidance, a white-haired man with a florid face. He stopped and followed my gaze out the window.

"They pass the babies around. I see 'em at lunch. It's a toy or a doll to them." He shook his head. "We've got twenty girls this year pregnant. We're getting public health involved. Taggert's gonna do something."

Amusement twisted his mouth. "Did you know that we have several students in the school whose mothers were students here when they got pregnant!" He gave a small laugh. "I mean, this school's only been open since the sixties, and we're getting the third generation!" His bushy white eyebrows rose quizzically. "They think this place is great!"

When I saw Jack's rusty orange car in the parking lot, I felt a shiver. He'd hardly been coming to class lately. I had tallied the growing number of absences, filled out the requisite forms. I had also been secretly relieved. The vehemence of his first poems, his death wish for the class, the switch-blade, that strange, diffident manner – he reminded me of the kind of young man the landlady describes later, in the interview with the news-paper: "Quiet, he kept to himself." The kind whose basement yields up gruesome photographs, or a cache of weapons.

A manila envelope dropped on my desk, and for one brief second a clammy hand brushed mine; then Jack's thin back moved down the aisle.

SOLNUKI was scrawled in inky, smeared letters on the outside: inside nothing but a piece of paper, folded. I smoothed out the picture, an advertisement of some kind torn from a magazine. Two women lay on the sand. The blond one, in a bathing suit, was stretching indolently on her back; the other, the one with dark curly hair, hair like mine, lay on her stomach. She was naked.

My insides clenched into a fist. I didn't know what to do. The picture on the desk – was she supposed to be me?

"I think Jack is trying to tell you to take a holiday in Jamaica this Christmas," Angie offered mischievously from over my shoulder. She held up the picture for everyone to see.

"Or something," Ray added suggestively. Across the class he gave Jack a lewd wink.

I stared at Ray hard to keep my eyes from moving to the seat by the window.

Jack had been away. But did he think about me when he was away? Was this an indication of how he thought about me?

The skin felt icy where he'd touched my hand.

■

From a journal:

> Today I am so upset. I think Im pregnant, and I dont have a clue what to do. I cant tell my dad cuz hell disone me, and I dont believe in abortions. I dont want anyone to know. Its Gregs kid cuz hes the first and only person I ever done it with. My docter wouldent let me go on the pill cuz he said you need your parents consent or you would have to be 18. Anyway, I am in a good mood cuz I got a front row and back stage tickets to see Megadeath. Im gonna party with them. there concerts are all guys to, cuz most chicks hate heavy thrash metal. Anyway, must go, by for now.

14

■

## THE PESSIMISTS

I hated rising out of bed into a morning that couldn't escape the night, driving home through a bleak dusk that the night was already swallowing. December kills. It devours the sun, the blue sky, spits out the bones of trees.

The feeling persisted as I reached into my mail-box. A photocopy of a newspaper article, "The Pessimistic Generation," awaited me. The vice-principal had clipped it, to bring to the staff's attention.

> The generation coming of age in the 1980s has lower expectations and self-confidence than their parents. They have seen family breakdown become commonplace and bankruptcy hit close to home. They do not trust politicians to improve their lives. In an age of . . . video-culture and fast-food relationships they are not sure where to turn.

Was it really so bad for them? I devised an assignment for the junior English class ("a simple, straightforward paragraph," I muttered wearily to Colin Beatty, whose shadow loomed over the class).

> I feel the world is realy truly rotten. Always the worry of nucular destruction. People starving in Africa. Killing in the Middle East. A large population of murders every where. Every morning you can't listen to the radio or watch

tv without hearing seeing feeling all the greif and distruction. Children being raped, abducted and brutily murdered. People dying because of bombs and crazy people with guns. When will it stop! Maybe not until death swallows us too.

Sinserely,
David

■ ■ ■

How can this world be good if racialism exsists?

Clive

■ ■ ■

On the news you always hear of suisides. There is over 3 suisides ever day and thats from jumping in front of the train. I seen them when I go on the subway there is so mony people wonting to die.

Bill

■ ■ ■

This morning you forgot to say hi, miss solinky. Well things can't even start to be great because problems keep coming. my mother won't leave me alone. She can go fuck-her-self. On top of that my father got hurt and lost his work and we have to move. That is the reson the world is bad.

Christie

■ ■ ■

I THINK OUR PLANIT IS FUCKED.

ANOMINUS

■ ■ ■

I think it,s a great world becaus of all the VCRs and stereos and video games and because of Heavy Metl and partys and other thinks like beatful women in nice tit black pantes and paper underware.

Kevin

■■■

I realy don't know what I think about the world –
sometimes it's great, or hell.

Let's start with hell. When there is war the world is
terible, you never know who is going to died or when. Or
when your neighbor has no job, then also the world is
terible. But to all this there is a good side, when you see a
baby being born, when your family and friends are happy
and healthy, when there's peace in this world and poltics
and religion are not upsetting anyone that is the great
part of this world.

Nadine

The narrow tables with the attached benches sat in rows against the cafetorium walls. White name-cards squatted stiffly on top. I found my name,
folded my legs uncomfortably under the table, and waited. It was Parents'
Night.

"Don't expect many parents," Colin Beatty had warned, when we
were let out early in the afternoon. "It's not the same as a collegiate – all
those mommies and daddies frothing at the mouth to make sure Johnny
gets into university." He smirked at Hilda Becker.

I straightened papers nervously. Beside me were my red Teacher's
Daily Record Book, my blue attendance binder, the three seating plans,
and a pile of returned pink Referral Room slips. Library slips, nurse excuse
forms, sign-outs, and sign-ins waited nearby.

Towards my fortress of paper limped a woman, leaning on a cane. She
placed it on the floor and settled herself into the blue plastic chair opposite me. "I'm David's mother," she said. She laid her hands on the table as
if they were reaching for mine. I couldn't help noticing that the cuffs of
her jacket were frayed.

"Oh. David . . . !"

"He thinks the world of you." She smiled shyly.

"He does? I like him too!" For a moment she was David in his desk at
the front, facing mine.

"He had such a hard time last year," she said slowly, shaking her head.

"A terrible year – at home, at court, at school. Me going in and out of the hospital all the time." Fatigue fell across her face like a veil. "But he's really turned around this year, and it's thanks to you."

"It is?" I laughed as happiness surged through my body like warm electricity. "Oh" – I pushed away the unlikely claim – "I think he just likes to write. And he writes well – he's one of my best students!"

She withdrew her hands and reached for her cane. "Well, I guess I should be going to see the teachers he's having problems with. There's that machine-shop teacher. He doesn't like that class."

Was it *really* true that I had made a difference? But she was already turning. The appliquéd polar bear on the back of her jacket, grey and bedraggled, moved slowly off.


Now a stocky man stretched out a strong hand. Milos's father, he said, in a heavily accented voice, resting his elbows on the table. Black chest hair curled from the unbuttoned throat of his white shirt.

He was a bricklayer, he told me. When it rained, he wasn't paid; when machinery broke down, he wasn't paid; when the economy went bad, no one wanted him. And now he had a son who didn't pick up a book, who was good with his hands. "I don't want him struggle to earn living, like me." He looked down at his callused palms, broken nails. He shook his head. "No future from this school. Electronics, computers – the future." He banished his working hands to deep pockets.


A small lady in a black dress, her hair invisible under a black kerchief, stood at the foot of the table. Beside her was a neatly dressed young man in his early twenties.

"My mother doesn't speak English very well," he smiled, helping to settle her small, thin body in the chair. "I'm her interpreter." His mother glanced at him apprehensively. "So . . . how is Gus doing?" he asked.

Gus? Self-consciously I searched the seating plans. "Oh, Gus! He's in my home-room." The mother stared back at me. A crucifix nestled in her black bosom.

She murmured something. Her son translated. "She says he is a bad boy." He smiled an embarrassed smile.

Her voice was firm in its foreign tongue. "She says he has bad friends." Three lines of worry pleated her forehead. "She says he has changed, this school has changed him. Before he was a good boy." She fixed me with her dark, anxious eyes.

Should I mention the water-pipe, or his daredevil stunt of lying down in the middle of the road? "I'm sure he'll be good again. It's just a stage that some kids go through," I said lamely.

The young man dutifully translated. His mother nodded, as if those hackneyed words, uttered by a teacher, had acquired profundity.

The interpreter helped her to her feet. "We should go now, find the other teachers. Thank you very much."

The mother nodded grimly, then moved off, her hand on the arm of her son. Her good son.


Two chairs scraped, a man and a woman sat. She was stout, with grey hair and a long, baggy grey coat; he was thin in his grey suit, under it a grey wool vest. "Hello." They had English accents. "We're Kevin's parents."

Kevin's mother! In my mind I had stood on the balcony of a high-rise, looking down with her at her fallen son. I had stood beside her in the prison waiting-room. Sat beside her in the courtroom when she heard the judge hand down the sentence.

"Kevin's parents! How do you do?" I restrained my arm from its automatic jerk towards the pile of pink slips. Instead, I pressed my sweating palm to a dry, chapped one.

"I understand you're a teacher," I said. She nodded. "How long have you taught?"

"Oh . . . ," she made a sound somewhere between a laugh and a sigh. "Twenty years. But one child, for twenty-four hours a day, is harder than all those little ones in Kindergarten. I expect I'll retire soon."

Did she mean from teaching, or parenting? "Do you have other children?"

"No." She paused. "Kevin is adopted. We adopted him when he was six."

That explained the mismatch. "That was something special, adopting a six-year-old!" I felt an urge to bolster the sagging body.

She didn't seem to hear me. "His mother was sick, then she died. He was in seven different foster homes. Then we got him." She looked at her husband, raised her eyebrows. Their faces were grey, too, like material that has been through too many washings.

"It must have been hard on him, all those homes!"

Silence. She shifted her bulk in the small plastic chair.

"What's . . . Kevin going to do when he graduates?" Another naïve comment, he'd be behind bars.

The father smiled apologetically. "Hard to say what his interests are. He likes, you know, video games, and his music. Though I've wondered sometimes what career can come from. . . . Well, but at least he has a hobby." A momentary light gleamed. "He doesn't read though," he added, the light fading, as if hope and despair played a musical variation across his face. "We're avid readers, we are. Mind you, he does look at magazines. Don't think he reads them, though." From its gully, the voice climbed again. "But it's good he has some hobbies, isn't it?"

"That is important, isn't it?" the mother added. Her hand fluttered like the broken wing of a bird.


Colin was right: most of the parents didn't come. If these same children had been lying in a hospital ward, as critically injured physically as they were academically, the parents would have been there, consulting with the doctors, wringing their hands at the foot of the bed.

Yet for those who brought their worried faces before me, what medicine could I promise? What surgery?


Leroy breezed through the door of home-room wearing a track suit partly unzipped, his chest exposed. "I'm leavin' tomorrow! Had enough of this shit!"

"Gettin' a tattoo," Gus announced. "A dragon. Told my mother it's my own money, she can't stop me." He looked around as if she might be lurking somewhere in the room.

Dori's head lay on the desk. "My family's splittin' up." Everyone turned. "My mom told me to get out. She packed her bags, called the airport. She's takin' my little sister and goin' back to Ireland."

"Then you'll stay with your father?" I said hopefully.

"He said, 'The kids can have the house, I'm goin' two thousand miles in the other direction.'" She sank deeper into her seat.

"But . . . where will you stay?" It was cold out now, grey and mean. Fall was surrendering to winter.

She lifted her head as if it were a heavy thing. "My friend said maybe I could stay with her for a while."

"You can get student welfare," Jamie suggested from the perch of his desk-top, before he dipped back into his bag of Fritos.

"Yeah, a hundred dollars a week," Sean muttered. "That'll keep yah in cigarettes."

"I wouldn't take no money from no fuckin' government!" Dori burst out. She raised her face. That's when I saw the bruise, its purple mottle masked by thick make-up. I wanted to ask her how she got it. But when she caught me staring, she buried her cheek in her arm.


Christie was waiting outside the classroom. "I'm gonna be missing English today. I'm tryin' to get an appointment at Guidance." She shifted her eyes away. They had dark circles under them. These kids went to bed so late, but what could you do? Despondently I fumbled in my purse for the key.

"My mother said maybe I . . . could get some . . . money, you know, for books and stuff." She followed me to the desk where I unloaded a pile of papers. She leaned against the blackboard. Suddenly I was aware that the slink had become a slouch. And where had the glitter in her eyes gone? "We . . . we're being evicted. At the end of this week."

Evicted. It sounded like "victim."

"My dad's unemployed. He's been tryin' to get Worker's Compensation." I'd seen her purple mouth sneer but never tremble. "We're goin' . . . downtown."

"I live downtown too," I said encouragingly.

"Not where I'm goin'." Her voice dried to a whisper. "It's a shelter."

"Gimme shelter! Gimme shelter!" the Stones had cried. It seemed to be the watchword of these kids: they were either rejected, kicked out, or evicted. They were the lost, wandering children looking for a home.

First I offered to drive Christie to the shelter, then I wished I hadn't. I'd just finished Referral Room duty, where ten kids had stared at me hatefully, between skirmishes, and I'd given thanks that the other ten hadn't shown up. Christie was waiting outside the door.

I turned on the car radio. Mozart would sing behind her words, secretly wash me in eighteenth-century order and calm.

"The sky is beautiful," I said. I scanned the wisps of rosy smoke in the west for balm.

She laughed shyly. "My grandmother and me, we see, in clouds, yah know, stairways with angels on the top." Was that when they were smoking marijuana together?

"So you moved on Saturday?" I watched the slippery road.

"I don't want to go there," she said.

My eyes turned back to the rosy clouds. I didn't want this conversation. I wanted to drive home all alone, let go of this day.

"It's not the movin'. I've moved about forty times. First we lived in the country, then a town, then the city, then from a house to an apartment." A series of moves, like a descending staircase, that ended at a shelter.

There seemed no choice but to talk. "How long has your father been unemployed?"

"He worked as a shipper. He hurt his back." Distractedly she ran her hand through her hair. It was reverting to its natural colour, I noticed – brown roots overpowering the green ends. Like December, the green leaves gone, nothing beside the road but tree skeletons.

"My father didn't get much grades, just to grade eight. He wants me to stay in school."

"It's a good reason for you to work hard, to get a good job." Behind her Mozart sang a song extolling discipline, steadiness, the regular beat.

"My boy-friend wants to be a truck driver."

"Is he employed?" Immediately I wished I hadn't asked.

"He was workin' in a factory, then he got laid off."

Something sat down on my chest, a feeling of fatigue, the weight of many people without hope, the weight of this long fall staggering to its impending wintry death. Sweet Mozart! I focused on the flutes.

We turned onto the highway. "Don't want to go there," she said, a refrain. Wordlessly we drove. Cars whizzed past, headlights jabbing the early dusk. Now the trumpets joined in. But Mozart had died poor.

"You know, the people there. . . ." When she resumed, her voice had picked up: "They're not the way you think they'd be. You think they'd be, I dunno. . . . But they're nicer than people, you know, with houses. They've been . . ." she paused, "through more."

I nodded.

"There's so many kids there! And that's another good thing, they take in anybody. Last night there was a couple with a baby. Nowhere to go, and they took 'em in."

Last night had been cold. For a minute I saw the young couple and their baby shivering outside a door. But it couldn't have been my door. In my neighbourhood on a cold December night only a few hardy souls wrapped in fur walked their dogs past those houses that sat like smug bankers warm inside their brick and stone suits.

"Only, there's the . . . cockroaches – I hate them things! I'm one of those people likes to take a shower in the mornin', and one of them crawled outa the drain." She laughed nervously, then was quiet.

I turned from the 401 south onto the Don Valley Parkway. Four lanes of tail-lights wound slowly south; four lanes of headlights wound slowly north. When I was a child I thought linked lights transformed a darkening highway into diamond necklaces and ruby chains.

"The people there seem sorta carefree," she said suddenly, "but, deep down, you can tell they're not."

I turned. Was this the Christie who had been so callous towards Clive, so insensitive to the feelings of others? But she had shown me the soft underside of the brittle skin before, when she first wrote in her journal: "I am so tired I could die." Now the words seemed prophetic.

"How can you tell?"

"Well, they leave their doors open, and when you pass by you see 'em sittin' in their chairs, like: 'Where's my life goin'?'"

I nodded. I knew that question.

"You know Florida? You ever been there?" Her voice rose. "We been to Clearwater. We had a place, went swimmin' every day. Did yah ever notice it's different there? You can put your problems to the side." She looked out the window. The last pink was falling off the horizon. "I wish I was in Florida now!"

Florida, the dreamscape. Once Ponce de Léon had searched its swamps for the Fountain of Youth. I glanced across: her eyes were far away, gazing on a shimmering sea. . . .

We pulled up to the side of a red-brick building. "That's our room." She pointed to a barred third-storey window. All the windows had bars. Was it to keep the residents from flinging themselves out? "I'll show you around," she said, leading me through the front doors, past a small plaque that said "Metropolitan Toronto Family Residence," past a bearded man with crutches, a woman changing a toddler's diaper on a brown plastic couch. Behind glass doors a number of adults and small children were eating at refectory tables. At the end of the hall was a counter, like a hotel reception desk. Near it, on the wall, hung a bulletin board.

"Thanks for the ride." Christie's voice came from behind. But my attention was caught by one of the notices:

> For women who wish to change their lives: Grant yourself
> another chance! Grant House gives women a second
> chance for a better life.

Was there a better life waiting for Christie? For Kevin, Dori, or Bill? Maybe someone could help them find a better life. But it wouldn't be me. I was worn out.

15

ONE OF US

"The most amazing thing happened," Bill exclaimed, his jeans soaked, the ragged ends of his hair moist.

"Bill." I took him by the shoulders and steered him to the cupboard. "Don't talk – *write*."

Journal day:

### MY MOST EXITING DAY AT SCHOOL

There was a coupla guys foolin around with the urinl in the washroom. They got the pipe off and when a kid come in they wud press were you flush and wud scwirt him. As they was doin this the pipe broke a great amount of water preshur came out and hit the kid he went flying back smack! into the wall.

The musty smell of damp wool emanating from Mr. Taggert's tweed jacket challenged the odour of mashed turnips. "Water, water, everywhere," he said, his voice cracking like the Ancient Mariner's. "Water on the floor, through the door, all the way to the tech wing." He stooped to wring out a cuff. "And I have no idea who did it."

I stared into the pale yellow turnips, trying to decide.

"Taggert just called me into his office. He was askin' who was responsible for what happened in the bathroom!" Bill gasped, entering class late.

Kevin looked up from the page we were checking over. "What'd yah tell him?"

"I didn't tell him nothin'!"

"Yah better not!"

"I won't! But who told that I was there? Who's the snitch?" My eye twitched.

Kevin's lip curled. "Yah better not rat. Some guy last year ratted, and he got both his legs broken. And the guy who ratted about who kicked the speakers in at the dance, he got stabbed. D'yah know what happens in prison if they discover yer a rat?"

My nose itched, but to scratch it was a sure sign of guilt.

"I'm not gonna rat!" Bill squeaked, oblivious to my nasal contortions. "But what'll I say when the police ask me who did it?"

If, at that moment, I confessed, they'd never write honestly in their journals again. Still, I had to tell someone. Desperate, I cornered Hilda Becker at the sink in the women's washroom.

"I was the snitch," I pleaded, blinking under the fluorescent lights that glared down on this chamber of female confessions. "But what else could I do? I have an obligation to the school. Right?"

"Never you mind," she said, her motherliness rising like warm dough. "It'll be a good lesson for him in Life Skills."

The vice-principal's voice boomed over the PA: "May I have your attention, please! This morning a student was found handcuffed to the urinal in the second floor boys' washroom. Anyone with information regarding this incident should see Mr. Taggert as soon as possible in the front office!"

"Principal at a collegiate, vice-principal for seven years before that, a graduate engineer, and a superb athlete," said Mr. Taggert, introducing the speaker at the front of the library. It was the last staff meeting before the Christmas holidays.

A stir ran through the rows of seated teachers like wind in grass. Beside me Nick Sawchuk had been ticking off the items on the agenda: number seven by 3:30, and only one left. "Go for the goal!" he whispered, seconds before the speaker was introduced. Now his pencil froze over number eight.

"I appreciate the fact that you're not interested in professional development just before your Christmas holidays," the speaker said, straightening his tie under his navy pin-striped vest. Nick's pencil wavered hopefully. "However, I am going to talk to you today about discipline and self-esteem."

"Discipline begins with self-esteem," he began. An overhead flashed on the screen:

> A positive self-concept is essential for a full, happy, productive and successful life. The problem is that schools systematically destroy self-concept.
>
> Benjamin S. Bloom

"One cause of that destruction is the way in which discipline is imposed by teachers," he said. "In my experience, ninety per cent of the discipline problems with students are caused by ten per cent of the teachers." He gazed meaningfully around the room. Beside me, Nick Sawchuk's pencil was boring a hole through number eight.

"Now, it's well known that discipline must involve logical consequences. For example, if a student goes to the washroom and stays out twenty minutes, let him make up the time after school. It is not a logical consequence to send a letter to his mother."

"What if he doesn't show up after school?" Nick called out belligerently.

The speaker nodded. "If he won't listen to you as a teacher, then the logical consequences are that he shouldn't be in your class. I would send him down to the vice-principal." There was a burst of derisive laughter. "As a principal, I would support that!" he added, defensiveness sharpening his voice. I glanced over at Mr. Taggert's drained face, his flyaway hair, as if at that very moment he had opened his door to the long line of students. "We wouldn't have anyone left in our classes!" Nick Sawchuk sneered.

The speaker raised his stylishly barbered head. He was a young man on his way up to the board office, and this response was unexpected interference.

He was from a collegiate. Maybe he just needed a little more information. I put up my hand. "Ah, excuse me." People turned, frowning. Questions were taboo, as they would prolong the meeting. "No one would dispute the idea that a positive self-concept is desirable. Highly desirable! It's achieving it that's the problem!" I shook my head ruefully.

"You see, it's just that . . . well, you have to understand the special schools. First, the students aren't particularly afraid of authority; second, they're often absent; third, their self-esteem is already so low, and they seem almost, well, *comfortable* with that. What I'm trying to say is that it's not always possible to apply logical consequences to a place that's not always . . . logical!"

I was collecting my papers in the English office when Colin Beatty appeared at the door. His tall thin body blocked the exit. Behind him, Hilda Becker blotted out the light.

"I liked what you said." He nodded slowly. "You're one of us, now."

The ceiling opened and a black cloth dropped. It fell about my shoulders and my head. I needed this holiday.

Dark as midnight when I forced myself out of bed. The shower jabbed my skin. Cereal lay in my mouth like wet clay. Grey oozed out of the east when I stumbled through the door, past the snow-laden oak, to the car. The gas gauge registered empty. If I was lucky I'd run out of gas on the 401. By the time the Motor League came the morning would be over.

The ugly, yellow, rectangular building waited on the hill, a cap of snow on its head, like an admonishing schoolmaster, its flapping flag a wagging finger. The driveway was a narrow channel, the parking lot a grey, salted sea. Cars chugged in, spraying slush.

A world of dim halls and low ceilings and corners sat inside that heavy glass door. Wordlessly I walked past strangers.

Jamie turned on a transistor hidden in his zipper bag, music ripping the nylon sides as if a rock group were trapped inside. Leroy assumed a boxer's stance and threw punches. He knocked off Jamie's hat.

"How was your holiday?" I asked by rote. My voice sounded flat. Behind it I heard Barbados: steel drums and rolling white waves.

Vacant looks. "I partied all week with my old man in Hamilton!" Jamie crowed. "Drank half a bottle o' beer an' fell asleep. My old man said: 'You committed a unpardonable sin, you left a beer unfinished.'"

Dori's head lay on the desk. Her blouse was the colour of the hibiscus bush that had bloomed outside my hotel window. But the blouse was wrinkled, her skirt stained, her hair surprisingly unkempt. "My mom has her plane ticket," she said.

"Things aren't better?" Christmas had come and gone, that time when I imagined families gathered around long, laden tables, sharing talk and laughter. But for Dori nothing had changed. Inside my shoes I stretched my toes, as if I were still on a beach chair, still lolling under a hot sun.

"Nope. I went home to do a laundry an' she started screamin', so I left." Her eyes were smudged with make-up and fatigue.

"Where are you sleeping?"

"On a stairway. Thought I was in my bed so I hung my arm down." She rolled up her sleeve to reveal dappled red and blue. Another bruise? The last one had been on her cheek.

The back stairway of some apartment building intruded on my paradise of waves and white sand: peeling green paint, cold metal banister, grimy steps. Should I offer to let her spend the night at my house? But what about my privacy, my family's? And what if she liked it there and didn't want to leave?

"Dori, you can't sleep on a stairway! Talk to Guidance, they'll help you find some place."

"They'll tell Taggert, and he'll call my mother. I'm not gonna get into that shit! I swear, if I can't get a job by next week, I'm gonna be a hooker!" She giggled.

"Where will you sleep tonight?" *Should* I take her home . . . ?

She shrugged. "I dunno. I'm gonna get stoned. Actually, I think I'll kill myself."

"I'm cli-i-mbing the sta-air-way to hea-venn," Jamie sang.

John burst through the door, his leather jacket unzipped, his skin below the cut-off jersey bright red, his belly button a shocked open mouth. "We don't have to come to school when it's this fuckin' cold! It's the fuckin' law!"

"For God's sake, do up your jacket! And wear a jersey you can tuck in."

"Don't look right." He blew on his red hands. "Hey, you got a tan. Where you been?"

"Barbados," I admitted reluctantly.

"You must be rich," John said. He didn't seem to expect a response. "How much money teachers make? They make good money," he answered, puffing into his hands.

Gus bounced up and down in his seat. "Went to the Roxy Friday night. Walkin' back along the bridge, really wasted! Saw some headlights comin'. The GO train." The bouncing got higher. "Fell off the bridge." Higher still. "Holdin' onto the ledge under the tracks, screamin' for help. . . . Good thing for that ledge!" he cackled.

"Gus." I stared at him from a great distance. "Why do you think it's funny?"

"Cuz I didn't die."

Suddenly something rang, like an alarm that jolts you out of deep, comforting sleep.

It was the bell.


"Write about your Christmas holidays," I said to the junior English class, an assignment so uninspired that it would surely meet with Colin Beatty's approval.

> **If the truth was told about Christmas holidays most people would say they are too long. I mean even after God finished creating the world he only took a day rest!**
>
> Clive

■ ■ ■

> **I feel sorry for the people at the shelter because theres a xmas tree in the lobby and the kids say look at the**

pretty tree can we have a tree of our own? And there
parents say We cant.

Christie

■ ■ ■

My family had a fight. They were discussin politics,
Brian Bulloney and the gang. My uncle called the police.
My granfather locked hisself in the washroom. He lost his
dentures in the toilet. Then he blamed Bulloney.

Bill

■ ■ ■

I had a very bad Christmas because my mother is
going into the hospital again in afew weeks for her 6th
operashun on her legs.

David

■ ■ ■

WHAT I DID ON CHRISTMAS BRACK WAS
  NOTHING NOTHING NOTHING NOTHING NOTHING
  NOTHING NOTHING NOTHING NOTHING NOTHING
  NOTHING NOTHING NOTHING NOTHING NOTHING
  NOTHING NOTHING NOTHING NOTHING NOTHING
  NOTHING NOTHING NOTHING NOTHING NOTHING
  NOTHING NOTHING NOTHING NOTHING NOTHING
  NOTHING NOTHING NOTHING NOTHING NOTHING
  NOTHING NOTHING NOTHING.

ANOMINUS

■ ■ ■

First we pick a place either my grandparents house or are
house but this year it was different we went to my brothers
apartment. My brother did the cooking he's realy good at
that. At exactly 12 midnight we open are presents some
people open there presents the next morning but we can't
wait. But there's some people who don't even have one
present, so before Christmas we try to give presents to

**people we know won't have a Christmas. That makes Christmas perfect.**

**Nadine**

Then they asked: "How was your Christmas, miss?"

"Fine," I answered vaguely. To them I was a privileged person – an insider. But I would never let them know how excluded I really felt at this time of year, passing the glittery lights that spangled houses, glimpsing the Christmas trees through curtained windows.

# 16

## DORI

The curly, dyed-blond head was bending over my desk in home-room, snipping an item out of the *Toronto Sun*.

"Are you back home yet, Dori?" Each time I passed my spare bedroom I felt jabs of guilt.

She held up the column she'd clipped of ads for rental apartments, some pencilled with an X. "Yeah, but not for long. My mom didn't go to Ireland, but I'm movin' out anyway. And quittin' school." She took a sip from my coffee cup. "My parents are bullshit. School's bullshit. I told Taggert to take his school and stick it!"

"I had nothin' to do with it," a deeper voice behind her said.

I hadn't noticed the construction boots with untied laces, the jeans frayed at one knee, the brown, layered hair. Even as I smiled at him, he continued to stare at Dori with concern.

"If you go, I'll miss you!" I was thinking of our intimate morning chats when she shared her muddled, troubled affairs.

We looked at each other.

"But I do remember when your birthday is." She grinned when I winced. Once, to my discomfort, some of the students had seen my driver's licence. Seen my age.

"So I'll be seein' yah!" she called back. She marched through the door, head high, ass twitching, her friend trailing behind, BRAD inscribed on the back of his black jacket.

Jamie and I looked at each other: home-room wouldn't be the same without Dori.

The familiar multi-ringed, stubby-nailed hand was reaching across the desk for my coffee cup. "Taggert told me to come back till the end of the semester. A few more weeks, *then* I'm leavin'."

It was Dori, all right, lugging around that life crammed with confusion.

She sat down on my desk. "Brad's gone to Myrtle Beach for a coupla days."

"Oh well, there's always Mike, or Dave . . . or Neil." Having her back made me happy.

She smiled at his name. "I spoke to Neil last night. First time I told him about Brad. Told him everythin'." She shook her head wonderingly. "He was so upset, he was bawlin'! I was bawlin' my head off, too! He said he's gonna kill Brad. He'd do it, too!" She smiled fondly at the thought. "But I been with Neil since I was twelve, I need a change. My mom wants me to get married with him, but I gotta go out with different guys before I settle down."

Her mom wanted her to get *married*? "How can you possibly know who you want to spend the rest of your life with? You're way too young!"

She giggled as if she hadn't heard. "Neil said he's gonna kill me too, then kill himself. God, we bawled!"

I looked at her flushed, smiling face, and suddenly the meaning came on an arrow: Those dark bruises, like the purple skin of a plum. Yes, the one on her cheek, then the one on her arm. He'd done that to her!

Dori stood in front of Jamie's desk, her back to me, as he gobbled his breakfast of corn chips and pop. "Come on, gimme some Pepsi," I heard her mutter. She reached for something under her rabbit-fur jacket.

"Dori?" Hastily she re-zipped the jacket and turned towards me. Something bulged on the left side. The anthem came on, and we stood in that odd position – Jamie's corn chip frozen in the air near his open mouth, Dori grinning sheepishly, I staring at the bulge.

"Let me see what's in there!" I said, the anthem over. "This is a bust," I added, trying to keep it light.

"*That's* a bust," Jamie interjected, pointing at Dori's well-filled sweater as she slowly unzipped her jacket and pulled out a Nescafe jar sloshing with amber liquid. Reluctantly she held it out.

I unscrewed the lid. The aroma of Scotch assaulted my nostrils.

"Well, don't *you* drink it," Dori said angrily.

I opened the window. The clean, cold air gusted in, and the scent of pine needles. I tipped the jar. The liquid trickled down, staining the snow like dog's pee.

Dori put her head on the desk. "What's going on!" I said.

When she finally raised her face, I saw that it was puffy and slack. "I been drinkin' all week. Comin' to home-room but not to any other class," she whispered hoarsely. "Promise you won't be mad at me? I took off one day, shot up coke."

*Coke? Cocaine?* The word shook me, the image of a needle piercing her white skin, invading her young veins. "I thought you didn't use drugs anymore."

Her body slumped forward. "Remember I told you how I was before Neil? That's how I am now." She looked up. I had a flash of her in middle age: straw hair and a potato face.

"Do you . . . want to come and talk to me after school?"

She smiled weakly. "Thanks for not reportin' me."

I guessed that meant I wouldn't be reporting her.


The folded piece of paper was lying in my mail-box under a pile of memos:

> Dear Miss Solnicki,
> I'm writing you cause I need to talk, and I trust you.
> I'm very scared and confused I don't know what to do I
> was thinking of taking off and going down to Halifax.
> I got friends down there, but I can't aford to. To be honest
> I was considering o'ding I still am I'm telling you this
> cause I'm so scared and frustrated. Brad fooled around on
> me in Myrtle Beach I really thought we had something

good but like usual I just got hurt. I'm tired of being hurt
not just by Brad but my parents and and friends too. Please
try to help me.

Love,
Your very best friend
Dori Murphy

p.s. This is just between you and me.


I was still thinking about the letter when she walked into home-room. A
brown cardigan slapped her sides; shadows bruised her eyes; dark roots
smudged her hair.

"I got your note." She wouldn't look at me. "Can I talk to you after
school? Will you come this time?"

"Dori Murphy to the office," the secretary's voice exploded out of the
intercom. She was on the list of truants.

Her face set. "I'm not goin'. If I go, I'll just scream at Taggert and he'll
kick me out."

"Don't go, then!" But she was on the blue Do Not Admit sheet. She'd
never get through the day. She'd never show up for our meeting.

"What day is this?" Jamie asked, checking his timetable.

"What month is this?" said Dori.


She sat on top of a desk, as if for a quick getaway, then looked at the
clock: 3:15. Brad's face peered through the glass in the door. She waved
him off.

"You look sad," I said, breaking the silence self-consciously.

"Actually," she spoke in a low voice, "I feel like a bomb."

"Dori Murphy, the bombshell." A silly joke. "So, you're pretty upset?"
The question hung awkwardly in the air. What I really wanted to say was:
WHY? WHY are you so screwed up? WHY are you so self-destructive? The
WHY kept rising and I kept swallowing it. She wasn't middle class, univer-
sity educated, Jewish. She hadn't grown up asking WHY.

"Brad went to bed three times with a girl at Myrtle Beach," she blurted.

"Is that what's upsetting you?"

"Well, somethin' else." She scrutinized the desk-top as if written on it in invisible ink were the answers to this mystery. "You know the name 'Cheri'? That was gonna be my little girl's name. She was gonna be born in December."

I could hardly hear her. I leaned forward. "You were pregnant?"

"The tube was, you know, around her neck. She was six and a half months."

"She was born?"

"No."

"When did this happen?"

"In September."

What was she trying to say? It didn't all fit. But the truth was in her eyes, brimming with tears.

"How do you know it was a girl?"

"I saw her. I went into labour. They left me, and I looked under the sheet. It was all formed. I freaked!" A tear rolled down her cheek. "A big black nurse smacked me, made me cry even more. I punched her back! She never came around no more." A satisfied smile pushed against the tears.

"You really wanted this baby?"

"I did! I did! And Neil was more involved than most guys."

Brad's face appeared again at the door. Again she waved him away.

"Dori." I moved towards her. "What about this OD-ing business?"

"I tried it with my mom's pain killers. I took ten. It wasn't enough. I just got sick."

Silence. More silence. Rhythmically she snapped her binder open and shut. Her hands were shaking. It made me cringe to look at the bitten ends of her fingers. "Listen, if you ever want to talk again, or write me another note. . . ." I stretched my foot until my toe touched hers. Was that a saline abortion she'd described? How much of what she had told me was even true? Maybe it didn't matter. I gave her foot another nudge. "And try to come to school more often. At least it's a place to come." I gave her shoe one last touch. I wanted to hug her, but I was a teacher.


Dori stood at the door, cheeks rouged, blouse pink, two leather-jacketed boys hovering like shiny dark leaves around a rose. Out of her purple plastic purse came two new duotangs, green and yellow. She began applying the labels.

Could our talk have made a difference? Pleasure radiated to the roots of my hair. Maybe this feeling was what made people choose the so-called helping professions, that reaching for an unpredictable hand instead of something solid and reliable – bricks, or a computer keyboard. True, the feeling could be snatched away at any time, but for now it was enough.

But already the blue Do Not Admit sheet cast a shadow. "You'll have to go down, Dori." She stiffened. "Listen, tell Taggert you're starting again – a new attitude for a new semester!" I was a cheerleader. "If he challenges you, tell him . . . ah . . . to speak to me."

She nodded. It seemed she actually believed in my new, self-appointed power!

Sleet scratched its nails against Mr. Taggert's window. It was only 9:45, but already he had the look of a cornered animal.

I held up the memo. "You wanted to see me?"

He focused, reached into a file, pulled out a card. SEEMS "REFORMED" was written across it.

"The way she talked about you, there seemed to be a connection. So I thought I'd tell you to hang onto it if you can. As far as I'm concerned, Dori's another one we've lost." His voice cracked.

"Listen, I think I should tell you . . . she wrote me a note." What if I didn't tell him, and something happened? "She was talking about . . . suicide." This door I had opened by receiving their confidences . . . and now I was responsible for a *life*! How could I have let that happen? "But I just can't imagine Dori taking her life – she's such a fighter," I added, pushing away the vision of her trembling, swollen fingers.

His pen stabbed a tower of pink Referral slips. "You may be the first person she's trusted in a while. She may be trying it out."

Trust. That scared me. I didn't want Trust hunching precariously on my shoulder like some big black bird. Anxiously I stood up, shifting attention to the wall behind him, to the photograph of the two wholesome, dark-haired boys. "Those your sons?"

He raised his red-rimmed eyes and nodded. "They're older now, thir-

teen and, ah, sixteen. I think." The voices outside grew louder, more restless. A body thudded against the door.


The muddy construction boots, the untied laces, the frayed jeans and
peeling leather jacket stood at the door of home-room. "Is Dori here?"

"No. Not for almost a week." I had seen her only once since she'd sat
in the front seat applying labels to new duotangs, putting a fresh cover to
her tattered life.

Brad shifted. "She's doin' bad things – a lot of drinkin', gettin' into
arguments with everybody."

"I wish I could help her," I said heavily. It was such a short time ago
that I thought I *had* helped her.

"Me too," he said, "but I can't even talk to her. We fight all the time.
She screams at me." We looked at each other disconsolately. The jacket
creaked. "I was on the bus yesterday, I saw her car at Neil's place. I guess
she wants to get smacked around, I mean if that's what she wants, cuz
that's what she's gonna get from him. . . ."

The jacket emitted one last plaint, then the scuffed boots shuffled
down the hall. BRAD disappeared around a corner.


"Miss Solnicki, this is Neil."

Neil had been brought to meet *me*? I jumped up from the desk,
acknowledging the event. "How do you do?" I reached out my hand. A
limp one received it, a pale, strained face smiled crookedly.

He was Dori's height, with long, sandy hair, light-blue eyes, uneven
teeth. I dug into his face with my eyes, trying to pry out the violence lurking under the cheekbones. But it was a regular face – a kid's face – that I
found.

Dori's cheeks flushed. "Can I have a sip of yer coffee?" She took a
bold gulp before I could answer, demonstrating her special privileges.
"When she goes outa the room I always finish her coffee," she laughed to
Neil, who was leaning a pair of crutches against the desk.

I looked down at the cast on his leg. "He was in a motorcycle accident," she said. "That's where I been the last couple of days. He got a

metal plate; doctor says he may never walk again." Her eyes glowed proudly.

"You must be in pain," I said.

"Naw, I'm takin' pain-killers," he said casually, as I strained to catch a hint of rage in his voice.

"What did you do?"

"Crushed my bone. In three months I start therapy, they have to teach me to use this foot again." He grinned. Was inflicting injury casual, too?

Dori studied the leg with proprietary affection. "I wrote somethin' on the cast. Show her." He hiked up his jeans. Lines of ink wobbled like veins across the white plaster. "It's a love poem."

Sweetness softened the contours of her wary face.

■

From a journal:

> Dear Jurnal,
>
> I'm seeing one boy for about one month now. I'm not interested in him anymore. But their is another problem. My old boyfriend (CLIFF) came to see me too days ago and he wants to start seeing me again. I wanna start seeing him but every time he's not around, I hardly think about him. He told me he wanted us to go out tonite but I haven't broke up with my boyfriend (PETER) yet. Well, they're is a reason I can go out with my old boyfriend (CLIFF) because my boyfriend (PETER) never been home since Sunday & never bothered to get into contack with me. I phoned him yesterday & he was their but he never bothered to tell me where he was. Also, I think I might be pregnant with my old boyfriends baby (LEONARD). Guys, eh? Well, I need help!

17

## I AIN'T GOIN' BACK

Why didn't they love reading? I had tried to establish a time for quiet reading. The result had been that the restless majority disrupted the cooperative few.

Maybe they just hadn't been introduced to books that would interest them. I made arrangements with Mr. Walpole, the librarian, and took the junior English class down for a Book Talk. Inside the library door was a display with the sign: TAKE ONE, THEY'RE FREE. These were the wallflowers of the shelves, books from a long-gone era when teenagers were of a different sort. Books with titles like *The Teen Girl's Book of Etiquette, God, Sex, and Youth, Albert Schweitzer: Genius in the Jungle,* and *Ten Secrets of Bowling.*

"Hope these ain't an advertisement of the rest of what's in here," Kevin said suspiciously, flipping through *'Twixt Twelve and Twenty: Pat Boone Talks to Teenagers.*

On a long table, as if they were being served up, Mr. Walpole had laid out a pile of new paperbacks, their covers emblazoned with pictures of boys in black-leather jackets, girls in tight jeans, motorcycles in shiny chrome. "These are High Interest," he muttered, buttoning the nubby cardigan over his belly, a pouting lip above his belt. We drew our chairs around the table and he began the Book Talk.

I was mortified when I took them back to class. "How could you throw around the cinammon hearts he was kind enough to pass out? And tip over your chairs? And crack jokes while he was reading? Why do you act that way around books?"

"Books is a nightmare, miss." Bill said.

> I don,t like reading. Like, it,s not interesting to me
> what other people do with their lives. Like who cares?
> People who right books must have some pretty sick
> minds.
>
> Kevin

■ ■ ■

> Reading is very boring. It puts me to sleep. I would rather
> wate untill the movie comes out. Miss Becker shows the
> movies. Why cant you do your class like hers?
>
> Christie

■ ■ ■

> IT BURNS YOUR EYES. THEN YOU JUST NEED GLASSES.
>
> ANOMINUS

■ ■ ■

> By the time i get half Throw a book i can't really remmeber
> What i have just Read in the Begging.
>
> Cammy

■ ■ ■

> Glancing through the books that are on the shelf
> hoping to find something that will interest myself
> Maybe this one! No that won't do,
> I'll probably read half and it'll smell like POO!
>
> Clive

■ ■ ■

> Following reading is usualy a book report to do on what
> you just read and if the words are to big you can't under-
> stand it and if you can't understand it how can you do a
> book report? But if you read it to us, then we would
> understand it.
>
> David

"Jill, give it up." Hilda Becker looked glumly up from a pile of papers. "They're here because they *can't* read. Otherwise they'd be in some other school. Show them movies. It keeps them quiet for eighty minutes, and afterwards you can ask questions. You know, they're so used to sitting tranquillized in front of the box. . . ." She sighed. "Personally, I have enough with getting through a day, making dinner for myself and the kids, cleaning up and going to bed. Getting up in the morning is what I call heroic. So why take on an impossible task?" She pushed the greying waves of hair back from her face and sighed again.

Hilda hadn't always been fat. Recently she'd confided in me that her husband, a businessman in Kitchener, had run off with his partner's wife. Kitchener had stayed in my mind because it's the centre of a huge delicatessen industry, and since then, whenever I saw her, I'd pictured salamis and summer sausages. It was after he left that she began to swell. Perhaps her sadness turned inward, and every sigh blew up her body more.

I stopped in front of a class set of books. The cover showed a picture of a black teenage boy leaning against a graffiti-covered wall. *The Contender.* "The gut-wrenching story of life in the black ghetto," promised the blurb.

"What's this about?"

"Harlem kid wants to become a boxer, but has to overcome the neighbourhood, the bad friends, his own discouragement – you know, the usual 'Big Dream' stuff." She began humming: "To dream the impossible dream. . . ."

I flipped the pages. Would they identify with a kid from a disadvantaged background? Find an inspirational message in this Cinderella story? Could it help break down some of that prejudice that was deep in their bones, as if they'd grown up with malnourished empathy?

And if we read it aloud, could we be finished in the little time left before the end of the first semester?

"Don't bother," Hilda warned, her hands falling to her desk as mine piled the paperbacks higher.

From the creative writing class:

BOOK

I feel as if I am a book
and every page is a diferent story.
The person reading me is a speed reader.
I want to tell him to stop
slow down
but he won't
he just reads faster and faster
and soon the book will end
and I will be placed on the shelf
with thousands of others
to be forgotin.
The dust will fall
the webs will form
and I will be
the memery of a book.

Angie


David's shirt gaped like a wound; three buttons dangled like popped eye-balls. He held his elbow gingerly.

"What happened!"

"Guy in machine shop kicked me in the knee, I told him to stop, he kicked me again, so. . . ." Carefully, he flexed his elbow.

"Is David Blane in class?" the intercom boomed.


He stood at the door, his jacket crumpled in his arms. His eyes looked enormous. "Came back to collect my books. I'm suspended for five days."

"Oh, David!" All those promises to himself.

But when he turned his face, did I imagine the flicker of a half-smile?


I was picturing her apartment as the phone rang: the polar-bear jacket hanging limp in the closet, the TV blathering on, and her, sitting in a chair; she would reach for the cane, painfully rise, hobble towards the kitchen. Maybe that was why the phone rang nine times before it was picked up.

"Mrs. Blane? It's Mrs. Solnicki. We met on Parents' Night."

"Oh yes," said a tired voice.

I sighed. "I guess you know David got suspended today. I just wanted to call and. . . ."

"Yeah." Her voice rose. "But the fight wasn't his fault, someone put a sign on his back that said KICK ME. He was provoked to throw the hammer."

"I see. But, still, it does seem, well, a pretty *extreme* reaction."

"I don't know if he told you that I'm waiting for a bed for the hospital again." The voice trailed off.

"He did mention something a while ago. Well, maybe that explains it. This last week David's seemed, sort of" – I reached for a phrase he liked – "out of control."

A short, bitter bark. "He's a lot better than he used to be. One time I went into the hospital he destroyed my house, another time he tried to kill himself."

"He did?!"

"Yeah, well, at least they know now it's real. Before their father died he used to say I was just doing it to stay off work. At least now they know doctors don't operate for no reason."

"Of course they don't!"

The voice warmed gratefully. "The one year I had no problems with my legs I managed to finish my grade twelve at Pearson, get honours in English. What I'm hoping for, when all this is done, is to be a social worker or child care – have a profession – you know, make something of myself. . . ." Her voice had become dreamy, rhythmic, as if this was an oft-told tale, a ritual.

How many others had used words like these? And all the time they'd been trapped in hardening resin like insects in amber. I felt a stab of recognition. I, too, had known the lure of the fantasized future. But at last there had come a time when I was fed up with the paralysis inherent in the dream, the waiting for someone or something to lead me out of it. That's when I finally understood that I had to break the spell myself. I picked up the phone. I got in my car. I went back to teaching. And I prayed that something old might lead to something new.

"Well, good luck with your operation. And if there's anything I can. . . ."

"At least he's got you for English!"

Discouragement smote me like a blast of wind. She must have forgotten: I was the one who had "turned him around." Some saviour I was!

From a journal:

> Dear Journal,
>     I baby sat over the weak end and I need your advise on something. Okay, I baby sat my cousin Amy and she's three years of age. About four times I felt like hitting her. How can I keep from hitting kids that I baby sit? Some times it feels I have to. Help!
>
> Signed,<br>Non ~~Violent~~<br>Vilent<br>or not?

"Miss, did yah ever do stupid things when you were young?" Kevin's shout from the back interrupted my loud reading. Around him heads snapped to attention; glazed eyes refocused.

I tapped *The Contender* against my hand. We would never finish it before the end of the semester. "Stupid things? How do you mean?"

"Y'ever break windows, or steal anything?"

"Well, maybe I stole a comic book or something once when I was little."

"A comic book! Har! Har!"

"Probably still rollin' papers with it."

"Rolling papers?"

"He means joints, miss," Christie explained.

"D'you know how easy it is to take furniture outa the Bay?" Kevin said. It was time for Tips for Shoplifters. "Yah go to Grand and Toy, buy those red SOLD tickets, slap 'em on, and carry the stuff out."

"Guy with a van comes to my neighbourhood," Bill said. "Seventy dollars for a Sony stereo. If it breaks, don't bother fixin' it, just get a new one. Want a stereo, miss?" he added.

"I can't believe people actually *pay* for stuff!" Kevin said.

"My buddy stole eight cars. Went to court. Only got three weeks."

"Stealin' cars is nothin'," Kevin said. "Long as yah don't bash 'em up."

"My boy-friend been to court five times – it's always dismissed," Christie said.

"When they put the cuffs on, yah keep turnin' yer wrist," Kevin instructed. "It makes cuts. Then when yah get to the station, show it to the chief. He tells yah to get lost cuz he knows the cop can get in shit." He hadn't been that cocky when I'd seen him get into a police car.

"Miss, did yah ever get into a fight when you was young?" Bill asked.

"I love it when girls fight!"

"Yeah. Meow!"

*The Contender* was about a fighter. I glanced down at it resignedly. "Why would I fight with someone? I mean, if I were upset, I would have *said* something, handled it with, you know, *words*."

I looked at their intent faces. They wanted to know more about me. "I guess you could say" – for a moment I had a strong urge to tell them all; but exposing myself would be bad for them, bad for me – "that I had a . . . well . . . a sheltered childhood."


How would they react if I told them about the ski trips to Mont Tremblant or Stowe every Christmas, the two months of summer camp, the piano and French horn lessons, ballet, figure-skating, horseback riding – this endless list of gifts?

Would they understand the silver dinner bell to summon the maid? The mandatory use of French ("Passe-moi le beurre, s'il te plaît")? The stories and plays my father read to us after the dishes had been cleared? The thick classics I crawled into bed with: *Lorna Doone*, *Jane Eyre*, Meg, Jo, Beth, and Amy . . . all the "little women" were my friends.

Would they understand the eagerness with which I came to school the morning after Parents' Night, knowing I would find my parents' proud comments on the blackboard? It seemed natural that they had left their mark: my parents and my school were allies.

And could they ever understand that the price of these privileges was Expectation: my father asking me, the youngest, my opinion on some world issue. Family and guests around the long dinner table stopped eating, waited for my small, stuttering voice.

Once, standing in the centre of the ring like a circus trainer, my father put me and our handsome chestnut hunter, Amigo, over jumps. I remember the feel of leather reins made slippery from sweat, thighs pressed desperately against flanks, the jump I stared at a long time before I leaned against the horse's neck. When it was over I crumpled to the dusty ground: the whole time I had been holding my breath.

I could never tell them this. I could never reveal our profound differences.

From a journal:

> It feels like years since me and my best frend have been "working" together hotwiering cars. We do it cause it's like a sport.
> Heres how you steel a car. First you take a slim jim slid it in by the handle then pull it up, second when your in the car you take out the egnition you cross the egnition and the starter wier's then it should start.
> I drive the shit out of them then sell the parts, and I have never been cout, and I started when I was nine.

"Do you have a few minutes?" The small body that appeared to have swallowed a basketball blocked the staff-room aisle.

That old reflex towards authority figures clutched my throat. "Sure," I said, with studied casualness. What was it? – my students' dirty poems? Their obscene plays? The noise from my classroom? I could see Mr. Pritchett and Colin Beatty huddled with the principal behind a closed door, their whispers rising like steam.

We sat down on the couch. "You'll be keeping your junior English class for the second semester. Colin Beatty thought you should teach them the Lit course this time." It was none of those things! The same juniors, creative writing – all familiar. "However, we've had to form an additional Special Education class, and we need another teacher. We'll give your home-room teaching period to Hilda. Would you be interested?"

"Special Education!" I sputtered. "But . . . I don't know anything about it." That wasn't completely true, though. I had taken a course called Special Education, Part 1, for five weeks at university one summer, I and hundreds of other teachers, some who took courses every summer to get accredited in so many subjects that they would never lose their position.

That summer I had chosen Learning Disorders as one of my electives. On the first day the professor had attempted to give us a definition of what we were about to study. Learning Disabilities, she had called them, or Dyslexia, Minimal Brain Dysfunction, Perceptual Handicap. There was this 10 per cent, maybe more, of all kids who were messing up functions like non-verbal integration, revisualization, perceptual constancy, figure–ground discrimination. . . . On that first day I wrote down what she said and put startled asterisks around it: "We don't know who they are, or what's best for them."

"I would consider it seriously," the principal was saying, as he uncrossed his short legs. That meant the conversation was over. "It's good to be teaching in a second subject area. At the end of the year it might make the difference as to whether you keep your job or not."


Possibly it was the first time the entire creative-writing class had all been together; it would certainly be the last. Angie, who had been away for weeks – communing, perhaps, with her dead father. Ray, his cartridge belt circling his waist like teeth. "Live," he grinned, touching the bullets. Of course he would fail, since, on principle, he had refused to write any poetry at all. And Jack. Since he'd delivered that picture of the naked woman, I'd shunned him. Finally he'd just stopped coming. But he was back today, sitting by the window, winter light sucking the life from his white face. I'd have to fail him too, though it scared me. What if he got angry and wanted revenge? What if the office made them retake the credit, and Jack and Ray turned up in my class again?

Some finished the exam after fifteen minutes; a few took longer than the hour. The papers dropped on my desk like white wings closing. I sat waiting, somehow hoping: "Thank you, Mrs. Solnicki, for leading us to a love of language, a love of poetry. . . ." They left without a word.

Only the Good News Bible Girl and I were left, just us and the crumpled-up papers lying in the aisles like the discarded shrouds of vanished ghosts.

"I discovered," she said, closing the Bible, "that once I start writing poetry, I can't stop!"

Something inside me lifted its head.

"And plays, I discovered I love plays!"

Sat up.

"D'you think I could take this class again next semester?"

Tottered to its feet.

"I'll . . . check into it." Then, inspiration tucked under her arm, she too was gone.

Ray's exam lay on the bottom. I would read his first, get the worst over with, I was thinking, as I opened to the poetry section. But I found POTRY IS FOR FAGGOTS scrawled in large letters across the page. Under it he'd left his insignia: F.T.W.

Fuck the world! Fuck him! Fuck them all! Miserably I turned to the exam on top:

### TEACHERS

Teachers are wierd
Teachers are crazy
Teachers are nice
Teachers are mean
Teachers are cute
Teachers are ugly
Teachers are a bunch of losers
Teachers are teachers
But God loves them anyway.

"Can I speak to you?" Christie's voice was urgent.

We went into the hall, away from curious eyes, and leaned against the lockers.

"Do you know if the nurse is here today?" Her once-impudent body seemed thin under the sweater, her hair and eyes dulled. The nervy, attractive girl of the fall had come apart, the pieces rearranged.

"I really don't know."

"I can't go back there tonight! Do you know any place I can go?" Tears welled in her eyes.

My spare bedroom would stay empty, I knew that.

"Guy next door, he's got scabies. And there's this virus – little girl I been baby-sittin', she's got a fever of 103, she was shakin', and the mother's pregnant, she's runnin' back and forth to see if her three other kids are okay." I could hardly follow. "I'm so scared I'm gonna get scabies!" she blurted. She stopped, her eyes wide. "What are they?"

Scabies. I'd come across the word when I was young; when I was reading about Anne Frank. I'd taken a book out of the synogogue library that told what happened to Anne, after the diary, before her death. In Auschwitz, a survivor recounted, Anne had been passed over during a selection for the slave labour camps, because she had scabies. That's when I heard the word. I was young. I remember thinking: If not for scabies Anne Frank might have lived.

"I'm not sure," I said carefully. "Some skin problem."

"Guy with scabies didn't take no shower for six months, till someone poured shampoo on his head. Said he don't believe in 'em. Thing is, I'm friendly with one of his kids."

"Tell the people who run the shelter."

"I did! Everyone did! They say they can't do nothin'." She wrung her hands. She was a similar age. Her world had been torn from her. She, too, had been taken to the limbo of the dispossessed.

Christie was looking down the hall, towards the front foyer, to where a bed might suddenly materialize. How many of us have felt that way at one time or another, stood with open, hoping hands for the bed, the boat, the letter, the money, the liberating army, the slip that dismissed us from a job we couldn't like but couldn't leave?

Her voice condensed into a cold whisper: "I AIN'T GOIN' BACK!"

18

■

# HOW DO YOU READ?

The vice-principal's voice boomed into home-room with a surprisingly renewed vigour that shook the chalk and the brushes.

"Welcome to the new semester! Let us take this opportunity to remind ourselves of the school rules, and to dedicate ourselves to turning over a new leaf.

"Number one. Only students whose cars have permits may park in the parking lot." He paused to let the first rule land. "Number two. No portable radios allowed in school." An electric twang shook the nylon casing of Jamie's zipper bag. "Number three." Gus signalled me over. "No smoking on school property." Out of his pocket Gus took a small packet, opened it. The inside flap said: "The best cannabis paper." "Number four. . . ."

"Take one," Gus offered. It was soft and smooth.

"Number five. . . ."

"Taste it," he urged. Tentatively I licked a coconut-flavoured sheet. He closed the cover, revealing the words "Made in Spain."

"Number six. . . ." I saw Spanish peasants hoeing rows of tall, green marijuana; they straightened their bent backs, shielded their eyes from the hot sun. Then they rolled a joint.

"Number seven. Alcohol and drugs will not be tolerated."

The new leaf was already going up in smoke.

I was almost late. I forced myself to move briskly down the hall towards the Special Ed area, pushed through the glass doors that closed behind me ominously, and drew a breath. I faced five boys seated at tables and chairs arranged on a rust-coloured carpet. At the back were scattered a few carrels.

Near my desk bustled a plump woman with long blond hair. "Ah, I suppose maybe I should . . . make some kind of introduction?" I whispered.

The aide nodded approvingly. "Say something about working on their strengths and their weaknesses in reading and writing," she whispered back.

"Ah. . . ." I cleared my throat. Five faces stared. "You have weaknesses." That didn't sound very nice. They *knew* they had weaknesses – why else would they be in this class? "I have weaknesses." Would that make up for my rudeness? "We all have weaknesses." It was sounding like a cheer extolling defeat. "And you're here to work on those weaknesses." That was more upbeat. "And you'll have success, because you have strengths as well as weak. . . ."

Five faces were looking out the windows, towards the hall, into the middle distance. A cloud of puzzlement covered the aide's face. I turned my back on the class. "I don't know what the hell I'm talking about!" I said under my breath.


The filing cabinets at the back of the room stood row on row, like highrises in a dense urban-renewal block. Beside them, like a landlady, stood the aide.

"You should take a look at these cabinets," she said, tossing back her long hair enthusiastically. "They contain our Programs."

Warily, I approached the labelled drawers: one said SPELLING PROGRAM, another CRITICAL READING, a third GRAMMAR PROGRAM, a fourth RFU. "What's that?"

From a drawer she took out a lime-green cardboard box, "Reading for Understanding" printed on the cover. Inside it, like a box of recipes, were stacked coloured cards. I read the first one: "Because Sarah's feet hurt, she took off her A. shoes B. coat C. toes D. hat."

The aide opened another drawer crammed with file folders dabbed with coloured chips. "The major headings are colour-coded yellow, and divided into Phases A, B, C, and D. Tests are orange, remediations blue, explanations green. The – oh, don't worry, you'll soon get the hang of it!" she added, observing that I was leaning against the wall. She reached out her hand. I thought it was to offer support, but it was to hand me a key.

The key to Special Education, the aide explained, was Strengths and Weaknesses. She suggested that I test each student to ferret out this duality, though what I would do with it once I had it was unclear.

Now, to my first assessee, a boy named Peter. He was sitting at the back, his pale, freckled face dazed, as though he'd just wakened from sleep.

As I leaned forward an unfamiliar odour assaulted my nostrils. I sniffed again. Then I knew what it was: human animal without benefit of bath. Acrid, pungent, much stronger than common BO, it must have been what our ancestors knew as the human smell.

We went over the questionnaire together. He had written that his least favourite subject was "English!" and his three wishes were "to be a chef, have a house, and to read." Class-mates, he wrote, annoyed him when they made fun of him.

"When do they make fun of you?" It was hard to hold my breath and talk at the same time.

"When . . . I read" – he stared straight ahead – "they tell me to hurry up . . . call me stupid."

About spelling, he had said: "I cant spell becaus I cant read."

What did that mean? "Yah got to be able to spell a word to be able to read it," he explained patiently, as if *I* were the slow learner. "And if yah can't read it, yah can't spell it." Had he just brilliantly summed up the Catch-22 of illiteracy? I peered into his foggy face.

Lastly, I handed him the piece of foolscap. "Write something about yourself and your life," I suggested, stepping back, gulping air.

He raised his faded, freckled countenance. "How do yah spell 'death'?"

The others eyed the new boy curiously as he shuffled into the room, a thin, reluctant figure who chose a chair, sat down, stared at the wall. He was transferring from a collegiate, according to the file. A truant officer had brought him in.

"Where have you been?" I asked. Silence. "We're almost a week into the semester already." More silence. My eyes followed his index finger as it traced an outline carved into the table, a swastika, one of several that I'd been trying to ignore.

He stared at the foolscap a long time before he wrote, slowly, painfully, as if the yellow pencil were a foreign thing:

ABUT ME

I am 15 im heir from larier colgate i hate sckol
I love muce plaing and dancing. I dislike my mom and
hate my dad i love wamen
The edn

"Sean, what does that mean?" I pointed to the second line, third and fourth words. Reading his writing was like deciphering code.

"Music playing." He looked down.

"Oh! What sort of music do you play?"

"Drum. Drum corps."

"Really! So you play in the drug corps, I mean, *drum*. . . ."

It rattled me to direct my questions to the top of an auburn head. "So, ah, you hate your parents? Do you live with them?"

"Uncle. Aunt." His hair flashed a warning amber light.

"I see! Have you lived with them for long?" My syrupy probing played counterpoint to his muffled monosyllables.

"No."

"Ah. And where did you live before?"

"Group home." His hair gave a final flop and closed him behind it like a door.

"Why don't you write something today?" I suggested. Sean's score in the reading test had been surprisingly high, higher than those of many of the kids who weren't even in Special Education. What would it be like to live with good reading and atrocious writing – as if one side of your body didn't match the other?

"Like what?" he muttered to the table.

"How about . . . school."

He half raised his head. "Anything?"

"As long as it's sincere."

"Can I swear?" He peeked up from under his bangs, then grinned at Peter. "Solnicki-picky." His face was handsome when he smiled. "Teacher-preacher."

"Teacher-creature from the deep lagoon," I added. Maybe he had a peculiar mental aberration and could only be reached through rhyme, like Lisa, in the book *David and Lisa.* "Write light, bright, not uptight," I offered tentatively, the way you might hold your hand out to a strange dog.

He looked at me oddly. "You nuts or somethin'?"

Maybe attempting to teach kids like him *was* nuts, I was thinking, as I watched him write.

### SKOOL

skool. skool is Boring to, to me anyway. I FUCKEN hate it so much i feel stuped ther. But you need a educashin or so they say

well that all i have to say to day

"Sean, what are the last three letters of 'singing'?" I was trying again.

"I-N-G."

"What are the last three letters of 'running'?"

"I-N-G."

"So how should this word be spelled?" I pointed to his composition.

"F-U-C-K-I-N-G!"

We exchanged a congratulatory look.

He was grinning over his 58, the third-highest test mark in Mr. VanBuren's carpentry class. "I told you you're not stupid!" I said.

He was so unusually positive that it seemed the perfect time to introduce him to a Program. But which one? From the top drawer of the nearest filing cabinet, under the heading LOGIC PROGRAM, I took a mimeographed sheet and put it before him on the table. "Let's do the first one together," I said. I read aloud:

> Mary got out of bed. She could not find her shoes.
> They were not under the window. Mary's shoes were
> under the bed or next to the chair. Mary's sister found
> her shoes. They were not under the bed. Jane found
> Mary's bathrobe, too. It was in the bedroom or in the
> closet. Mary's bathrobe was not in the bedroom.

I stopped. I knew I had read it, because I had heard my voice. But *what* had I read? "Now," I said, covering my confusion, "you have to circle the right answers to the questions."

> a. Mary's shoes were next to the chair.
>    TRUE     FALSE     NOT SURE
> b. Mary's bathrobe is red.
>    TRUE     FALSE     NOT SURE
> c. Mary's shoes are not black.
>    TRUE     FALSE     NOT SURE
> d. Mary's bathrobe was in the closet.
>    TRUE     FALSE     NOT SURE
> e. Mary's shoes were not next to the chair.
>    TRUE     FALSE     NOT SURE

"This is dumb! Who cares about her shoes? Burn em!" Sean scowled.

"Let's try the next one," I said brightly. Maybe we just needed to get away from Mary and her bleary early morning bungling.

> Bill goes to George Washington School. Bill is six or seven
> years old. Dan is Bill's friend. Dan is in Miss Craig's class
> or in Mrs. Benton's class. . . .

But Sean's head had begun its fall, and neither Mary, Jane, Bill, Dan, Miss Craig, Mrs. Benton, nor I could stop it.

Peter looked disdainfully at the book on his desk. "I don't wanna read that dumb book!" It was one of a series for slow readers – the print big, photographs for illustrations, only a few sentences on each page. He held up another book. "I rented this from the library. It's called *Never Cry Wolf.* Can I read it?"

I raised my eyes from the filing cabinet drawer, and nodded.

He opened it to the first page. He lowered his head. He raised his head. "What's this word?" he said.

I came over. "'Formidable.' It means hard to overcome, as in 'a formidable task'." I was developing a technique of shallow breaths that circumvented the nose entirely.

"What's this word?"

"'Sojourn'. It means to stay, as in 'to stay at a hotel'."

He laid his head on the table as if these words weighed him down.

"Peter, maybe it's too hard. That's an adult book, you know. There are other. . . ."

He studied the picture of the wolf. His hand moved across it. "But I wanna read it! I saw the movie, and I wanna, you know, comparison it!" His fingers pressed deep into the wolf's silver fur.

If only I knew how to teach him to read! "Maybe, if you start with easy books, and work your way. . . ."

His fingers clenched the binding. "But if you keep pushin' and pushin' it with the hard books, maybe you could do it! Maybe you could suddenly read!"

"I'm . . . not sure, but I don't think it works that way." But how did a person learn to read? Wasn't it supposed to happen in grade one, that explosive moment when all those inky blobs and sticks suddenly meant something, like Archimedes in the bathtub. All those ideas and images, stored for hundreds, for thousands of years, suddenly spilled out, like jewels from a velvet box.

"Do you have any ideas for helping someone learn to read better?" I asked the aide. Why had Peter been neglected? Why had no one matched him with the right Program?

Her blue eyes shone. "Well, let's see . . . there's Critical Reading; that's for reading comprehension. Then there's RFU; that's comprehension, too. And there's Word Wheels, and Three Minute English, and Cloze Procedure, and the Dolch Program, and USSR, that stands for 'Uninterrupted Sustained Silent Reading'."

I stopped her. "Has he ever tried any of them?"

"Of course! He's in grade twelve. He's been doing all those Programs for years."

■

From a journal:

> I just don't understand. I only missed 12 days exsept for the suspensions and most of my assinments were in. And I only got 59%. Nadine missed 9 days and got 87% I don't think that's fair I participate in class discushions and I'm not a shit disturber I'm there I do most of my work and I get a shity mark. Your're picking favorites that's not fair either. Now there's another semester that we have to have this class! I think I should give up school I've got enough problems as it is and I don't need teachers or principle getting on my back. So fuck english I don't give 2 shits!!
>
> David

19

# I AIN'T NEVER GONNA READ

"Undercover cops, miss." I and the rest of the junior English class crowded around Kevin, our breath steaming the cold window. I wiped a clear patch then looked, past the snow-laden pine trees, down the trampled steps, to a small blue car parked in the front driveway. Two men sat in the front seat staring straight ahead. From a distance I could make out short hair, protruding ears, thick necks. "If yah see 'em, yah should always try to ram their car," Kevin advised, "'cause they can't get insurance."

I rubbed the fogging circle. "How can you tell they're cops?"

"You can just *tell!* Anyone can tell!" They all agreed it was obvious.

"Remember, she said she was sheltered," Bill said.

As I ushered them back to their seats, away from their vivid, violent, real world towards a fuzzy, safe, book world, I wondered how much about me that word had revealed.

"What do you think 'sheltered' means?"

"Everyone sits down together at the dinner table and yah eat from the four food groups."

"Yah open the fridge and it's full."

"You play with yer dog every Saturday which is well groomed."

"Yah sit in class every day and pay attention."

"Your father meets the guys yah go out with, and asks 'em prepared questions. They haveta fill out a application form."

"It means yer a yuppie."

I winced. "Why do you say that?"

"Yah got snazzy outfits and millions of belts."

"I bet she drinks that bubbly coffee with specks in it from Italy. *Cap-a-Gino.*"

My laughter masked my dismay: They weren't far off!


"I'D RATHER BE HIGH," said the button still pinned to Randy's leather jacket. He was sitting in front of me in the small conference room that opened onto the Special Education work area. Three months ago, Randy had been the one who had helped Kevin unjam my classroom door.

The school kept trying to integrate him into regular classes. But the reports in my hand indicated that he was slithering into the twin troughs of "absenteeism and unacceptable behaviour." It was my job to communicate these observations.

He was sliding a Kleenex box back and forth along the table; past me went the filthy nails, the nicotine-stained fingers. I held up the comments for him to see. He shook back his hair, greasy drapes that parted to reveal pimples erupting on his nose and chin. The teachers were the ones at fault, he sneered. The pace of the Kleenex box picked up.

"Maybe you'd rather be high," I said, reading his button.

The Kleenex box stopped abruptly. "Yeah!" he exclaimed, "I work better when I'm high. Concentrate better."

"Gee, maybe you should come to school high every day. *High* school," I teased.

"Thanks for the permission. Yah got the money?"

I smiled benignly. "You still friends with Kevin Smythe? When I was taking my home-room class to the museum, we saw you guys walking down the street. Where were you going during school hours?" In my mind I still sometimes saw Kevin's grey, washed-out teacher-mother. I worried with her about Kevin.

The Kleenex box did a little dance. "Oh . . . just some business." His grin revealed crooked front teeth; they leaned against each other like two good friends.


How ironic that the students most in need of help were the ones most often absent. Only Dino turned up every day, nattily attired in button-down collar and leather tie, his black curls stiff with gel. Maybe that was why I muttered to the aide: "What's the good of all your Programs if there's no one to program?"

On the twentieth ring the phone was picked up. "What!" an angry male voice shouted.

"Is Randy Edwards there?" I asked.

"If one more person wakes me. . . ."

"I'm sorry."

"Phone's been ringin' all morning." The anger was softening to gruffness. My confidence rose: I had a right to call – I was a teacher.

"Well, if Randy got to school more often, maybe fewer people would wake—"

"Who is this?" the voice said suspiciously.

"Mrs. Solnicki, Randy's Special Ed teacher. Who are you?"

"His brother. My cousin just come over – booted him outa bed."

Now I was getting facts. "Why does he sleep in?"

"'Cause he goes out."

"Until what time?" I was warming to this conversation.

"Ahhh," the voice growled. "My parents think he comes in around eleven. They go to sleep, he's home two, three in the mornin'."

"What's he doing out so late every night?"

"Oh, smokin' dope an' drinkin' beer, I guess. Can't do nothin' about it. Useta smash his head in, he just goes out and does it again. But if he takes my motorcycle one more time I'm gonna kick his brains out! He don't have no licence or insurance."

"How old are you?"

"Twenty-three."

"So how come *you're* sleeping in?"

Lillian, the assistant head of Guidance, swung around in her chair. "Well, Sean, we want to help you, but we can't help you when you're not coming to school, can we?" Her jaunty English accent bounced off the walls of the small office, off the framed photograph of her fat, smiling baby.

Sean studied the floor.

"*Can* we?"

Barely audible. "No."

"You did miss a lot of classes at Laurier, but now you have an opportunity for a new start. So why not come to school? Don't you like us? Is it something we've done?"

Mary's shoes, I thought. Horrible Miss Craig.

"I . . . don't know if Sean minds my saying this, but he did write that he feels, well, stupid at school." I looked to see if I had trespassed, but there was no answering stop-light from the crown of his head.

"How long have you felt this way?"

For a second he raised his eyes. "Grade one," he muttered. *That* long? Hate kept that long was a friend!

"And what makes you feel stupid?" she asked. "Do you feel stupid in your shops?"

"Not in the practical." He'd strung four words. I felt hope surge.

"Is it the written, then?" A nod. "With taking notes?" Another nod. "At the beginning of the semester the teachers give a lot of theory; then it gets more practical," Lillian answered the silence.

Once I'd asked Sean to copy something from the blackboard. I'd watched him take down one letter, look up, take down another. "Try to say the word in your head," I'd suggested. "That way you can remember it, and you won't have to keep looking up." But he couldn't do that. He was a musician, yet he couldn't hear the word. Why?

"I'm going to check with your shops," Lillian was saying. "Maybe there's some way we can get around these notes."

"Speak to Mr. VanBuren; Sean has him for carpentry. He's a nice man, he'll help," I said urgently. If we could solve the note problem, maybe Sean would come to school; then, maybe, I could help him to write.

"Does your mother know you don't come to school?" Sean's gaze plunged.

"He . . . lives with his aunt and uncle." I glanced over guiltily.

"What time do they go to work? Sean?" Her voice nudged him.

"Eight-thirty."

"Do you go out the door with them?"

The top of his head moved imperceptibly.

I leaned forward intently; now we were getting to the heart of it. "Where do you go?"

"Sauna," came the whisper.

"What do you do in *there?*"

"Play drums," said the whisper.

"Isn't it a bit hot?"

"Outside . . . weight room," he breathed, as if I were extracting secrets through electric prods.

And suddenly I could see him, beside the metal body of the Nautilus, near the wooden sauna doors, tapping the long hours of the windowless day, tapping loneliness, boredom, the feeling of being stupid. Little Drummer Boy.

"I'm going to talk with your teachers, see what we can do to make it easier for you. I'll let you know at three o'clock. Will you come back then?" But no answer slipped out from behind his hair's bronze wall.

I opened the textbook from Special Education, Part I, that brief summer course I had taken, and, sighing, read the first sentence: "There is presently a deep concern over how to teach children who have near-average, average, or above-average intelligence, but who have difficulty in learning. Although the basic integrity of their sensory input systems, such as auditory and visual acuity, is within normal range and their speech and motor performance are adequate, the children do not learn at a normal pace. . . ."

But it wasn't only Sean, Peter, Randy. They might be the more extreme cases, but in everybody's classes there were kids with problems. Mr. Taggert had recently dropped the startling statistic that up to 90 per cent of our students had received some Special Ed assistance in elementary school.

I was reading, re-reading – but the words had begun to blur. Soon only certain sentences and phrases were surfacing. "Multidimensional phenomenon. . . ." "Auditory, visual, or tactile-kinesthetic processes not synchronized. . . ." "Intra-channel disorders. . . ." "Learning modality. . . ."

A phantom – the author of the book, no doubt – had crept up behind me and clamped a vise to my head. Was this what my students experienced when I saw them abandon a book, lay down their heads? I forced myself to go on. "Decode the students. . . ." "Open channels. . . ." "Utilize contributions . . . medicine, psychology, social work. . . ."

The vise was tightening. How was I supposed to apply all this, eighty minutes a day, five days a week, between two other classes?

I shut the book.

Sean, I was thinking, as I laid down my head, this is the Eureka moment when I have deciphered the meaning of the coded message you drum to the walls.

*Handbook of Special Learning Problems*, chapter four: "How to Deal with Children Who Are Having Problems Learning to Read." Among the baffling headings suggesting Dolch Lists and Configuration Clues, a reassuringly simple one jumped out: "How to Teach the Use of the Dictionary." Under it the author expanded: "We have encouraged youngsters to browse through their dictionaries when they have a few minutes to spare. They report having enjoyed the experience. One day we heard a young man exclaim, 'That's how you spell "abacus"? I always thought it had a "K".' He'd learned something, and been pleased by it."

I put down the handbook. Randy was aiming elastics at Dino's head: he was a youngster with a few minutes to spare. "Randy, here's a dictionary. Why don't you take a look at it?"

He turned it over in his hands as if it were an official envelope that brought bad news. Cautiously he opened it, and a surprising look of interest crossed his features. Before long he had hailed Dino, and the two of them were hunched studiously.

What a beautiful sight! If only the principal would walk by: in his vest pocket the Complaint would shrivel! And this could only enhance my prestige with the aide, whose behaviour, of late, had been cool. My teacher's heart swelled. Language meant so much to me; were they, too, learning to love words?

I tiptoed up and peeked over their shoulders. Which word could possibly give them so much pleasure? My eyes skipped down the page.

"CU . . . CUN . . . CUNT."

"Is anyone gonna hear this?" Peter asked suspiciously from the door of the conference room, as I explained the plan. He squinted at the tape recorder sitting on the table.

"Just you and me. The idea is that you read into this, and then, I'll . . . well, I'll understand what your mistakes are. Your, ah, *miscues*, actually.

And you'll hear yourself, and you'll hear your mistakes, too. Your *mis-cues. . . .*" I'd found the technique in a Ministry of Education pamphlet.

"I already know how I'm gonna sound," he muttered glumly. "Dumb."

"If you'd feel more comfortable, I'll leave you here alone."

He looked dubious. "You sure none of the guys are gonna hear this?"

"Of course not," I reassured him.

"Well, let's play it back!" I said brightly, closing the door. "Now you'll be able to learn from your . . . *miscues.* Here, let's follow along together where you read."

Oh, the starts, the stops, the stammers, the mangled words, the over-looked sentences, yes, sentences actually leaped over as if they were obstructions on a rocky road to a dead end.

"Yah see!" Peter brayed, startling me. His face flushed deep red; patches spread down his neck. "I told yah I couldn't read for shit! I ain't never gonna read!"

The vice-principal's voice boomed over the PA: "May I have your attention, please! A visitor to our school left a silver 1987 Chevy Beretta on the driveway with the keys in the ignition. When he came out he found the car across the street, smashed against a telephone pole. Anyone with information regarding this incident should see Mr. Taggert as soon as possible in the front office!"

■

# 20

# DEATH SPEAKS

Ray was heading down the hall with three friends as I turned the corner on hall duty. My anger rose. By failing him and Jack on the exam, I'd ushered problems back through my open door.

"Ray . . ." I called. "Where were you last period?" Their backs continued down the hall, in their hands no passes visible. "And where's your pass?" Their pace quickened, but so did mine. When they came to the intersection near the Special Ed area, they slipped down the corridor that led past a fire exit. "What class are you supposed to be in?" I called out. Students leaned against their lockers, giggling. At least border guards had the aid of radios, helicopters, machine guns. "What are your friends' names!" I demanded.

One of them looked back and flashed a greasy smile. "I.M.A. Dick."

Ray smirked. "U.R.A. Cunt."

From the exit I could see them racing down the driveway, their loud laughter trailing behind, a mocking banner.

I spun around and stomped down to Mr. Taggert's office.

Sean's uncle stood to shake my hand – it was his turn to be summoned to deal with the Sean problem. He was a tall man in his thirties, wearing a beige shirt, brown polyester pants – some kind of uniform. Behind him, as he told Sean's story, the snow gazed back blankly through Mr. Taggert's window.

First there was a stepfather, then the mother had a boy-friend, and by the time Sean was eleven the mother didn't want to look after him any more. For two years he and his sister didn't attend school. No one seemed to care.

Then the uncle took him in. Not really an uncle, but the husband of a woman who had been a foster child of Sean's grandmother. Under this new wardship, in this confusing cycle of child-care, the children returned to school. Driven by their hopeful guardian to the front door, they often went straight out the back. Finally, Children's Aid took over.

Again the so-called uncle and aunt took pity. If Sean would only attend school, he could return to live with them. Otherwise he would be out on the streets. There was still hope for him, the uncle said; the older sister was a lost cause, gone to welfare for good.

Mr. Taggert interjected. It was time for firm action of the administrative sort. He outlined Plan A, Plan B. If those didn't work, he'd call on Plan C. He punctuated each plan with the sharp poke of a pencil into the omnipresent pile of pink Referral Room forms.

The uncle rose, scepticism evident in his slack handshake, his sheepish smile.


The pork chop, Today's Hot Entrée, stared up from the plate at Mr. Taggert like a brown, baleful eye. Three days ago he'd confidently made plans, but since then Sean hadn't turned up. And Sean wasn't the only one. Large numbers of students in the school were absent every day. Sometimes the Absentee List, compiled on long white sheets, ran for two pages. Where were they? At the Eaton Centre? Watching the soaps? Getting into trouble? Working? Sleeping?

"Of course, it's worse in the special schools," he muttered, "where we have more kids dropping out. But it's everyone's problem. The Scarborough Board handled five thousand truancy referrals last year. So what are the numbers across the province? The country?" He cut a slice out of his pork chop's accusing eye. See no evil, I thought. "Before 1985, students sixteen and under could be prosecuted under the federal Juvenile Delinquents' Act." Hear no evil; I fought my urge to tune out. "Now" – he chewed thoughtfully – "since the Young Offenders' Act, chronic skippers *can* be taken to court. But there's no penalty for failing to comply. And there's no direction from the ministry. No one really knows what to do – not the judges, not the social workers, and certainly" – dejectedly he shook his head – "certainly not the vice-principals."

Somewhere, buried under those numbers, was Sean, his voice calling ever more faintly.


A student burst breathlessly into the creative-writing class. "Kid with a Kango outside school before home-room wavin' a hundred dollar bill! Then he ripped it, said he'd give half to whoever'll punch out his girl-friend. They get the other half when it's done!"

"Said he was gonna give *two* hundred to cut her face!" someone else added, "so whenever he saw the scar he'd remember what she done to him."

"What'd she do?" A voice rose out of the mesmerized stillness.

"Broke up with him."

Ray's voice broke in: "That's sad. . . ."

"You're not kidding!" I seconded energetically.

". . . that he can't beat up on his girl-friend himself!" he finished.

My eyes homed to their magnet, last seat, fifth row, by the window. Jack had his knife out. He was cutting, cutting the desk's skin.


Although Angie was no longer in my creative-writing class, we often exchanged smiles in the hall. Today she stopped me. "Miss, can I still show you things I write?" Her eyes held mine.

I hadn't forgotten her description of the violent way her father had died, or that she wrote to him every night. I nodded.

She reached into her purse, brought out a creased sheet of paper. It smelled faintly of perfume, the way a room retains the trace of someone who has left.

### DEATH SPEAKS
### by Angelene Billet

The night was black as velvet outside her bedroom window. She sat up on her bed wide awake. For she had heard it. The voice of death.

Yes, it was coming from the walls of her bedroom. Death was speaking to her. But she was not afraid. For she spoke to death every night after everyone had gone to bed.

She knew of all who died and of all who will. For death told her who will get the next message.

She had never seen death. But she knew his voice well. The voice of death was like a melody.

Every night she spoke to death until finaly sleep came over her.

Each morning when she had awaken death was gone. So she got ready for school and never stayed for breakfast. If she did she would have to eat with everyone else.

She prefered to leave when everyone in the house was still asleep. Every time when she did awaken late she was forced to hear the shouts of her mother's boyfriend.

Every time he saw her he had to yell at her or call her a bitch. As if he wasn't hole unless he put her down.

She lived with her mother and her mother's boyfriend because when she was thirteen death came for her father. After that she was living with her grandmother then death took her away to. Now she was waiting for death to take her mother away.

In school she was a cheerful student and no one could ever guess her tormint.

21

THE REAL ME IS

GONNA BE A SHOCK

Every time I lifted my eyes I saw Ray's scowl; every time I turned my head I heard his jeer. His presence at the back of the creative-writing class was a shadow, a reminder that, like him, I had failed.

Then, one day, I had an idea.

I was handing out the journals. I walked down to his seat. "Ray?" The chains on his jacket clinked menacingly. "I know you're mad at me. And you can't tell me to my face, because then I'll have to kick you out. However" – I spoke to his sneer – "you're allowed to say whatever you want in your *journal*." I dropped the unused notebook on his desk.

Journal day:

> Miss your such a fucken dork you had no reason to
> report me to Taggert and I got suspended. When I
> called you a cunt in the hall it was only ment for a joke.
> I thought your a bitch but I don't worrie about it now,
> whats done is done.
>
>                                 Ray

The creative-writing class was practising the cinquain – a simple five-line poem.

The problem was that the students didn't know their parts of speech.

After I had given them a quick, ineffective grammar review, they chose their own topics:

Father
big, strong
Drinking, hitting, sobbing
Never would slow down
Nobody

■ ■ ■

sex
loving, meaningful
sloppy, sweaty, exciting
I am in heven
whew!

■ ■ ■

girls
smart, snekey
play, talk, leave
should be shit on
boyes

■ ■ ■

knife
sharp, pointed
slash, cut, mutulate
use as a weapon
saber

■ ■ ■

Jesus
kind, sweet
loving, seeing, helpin
a realy neat guy
Christ

■ ■ ■

Taggert . . .

I hesitated. Was it professional for me to read out unflattering descriptions of my colleagues? But the class's urging made me go on.

**dickhead, Asshole**
**gay, bugging, obnockshus**
**always bein called down**
**Target**

I stared at the poet's name, and a thrill rang through me like a note of music. Carefully I glanced down row one. He was sprawled low in his desk, aiming his forefinger, crooking it as he squeezed the trigger. When he caught my eye, I nodded. A slight movement – after all, the poem, if discovered, would definitely become a Complaint – but a small nod to Ray just the same.

I spoke out my own name before I realized the last one was about me; then I clammed up. But the students goaded me. Blushing, I continued:

**Miss Solnuki**
**gorgous, fair-eyed**
**playingful, helpful, understanding**
**a sencitive teacher**
**sexy**

Their hoots and laughter fanned my face. But they didn't know the real reason why it flamed, or why my hands fumbled and almost dropped the pile of foolscap, or why I stood, speechless.

It was the smear of heavy letters, the words smashing across the paper like waves rearing headlong towards the fearful watchers on the jetty; though the poem was unsigned, I had recognized the writing.

This was Jack's poem.

Yellow, orange, fuchsia, mauve, jade. . . . These cards, these multiple-choice questions, these Programs that glowed deceptively like artificial flowers deep inside the cabinets – what was their purpose? Once, maybe, they'd been part of someone's step-by-step vision. I knew what they were now: busy work!

What was I supposed to do? I didn't have the resources to follow the textbook's suggestions; and, anyway, I didn't want to look at language that way, under a microscope, poking at it with a cold, metal instrument!

Were Randy, twitching restlessly in his seat, and Dino, and Peter so very different from Jack, a so-called normal student? Why shouldn't they be allowed to write too? And dream! Yes, what was writing, really, but a spinning of the mind's flax, a shaping of something tangible from wisps of thought, feeling, dream?

What had finally unlocked Ray but an act of self-expression? Why not these kids?

I glanced at the aide and cleared my throat. "How would you like to make some changes in this class?"

"Yeah! Sex, drugs, and rock 'n' roll!" Randy hurled another pink eraser chunk at Dino's head.

"No more 'USSR': Useless, Stupid, Shitty Reading," Dino added, ducking.

"USSR stands for Germany, yah dumb dick!" Randy said.

"How about a better-lookin' teacher?" Peter's attention had been recalled from the window. "Yah seen today's Sunshine Girl?"

"No way. Miss Solnicki's a pretty teacher!" Dino's smile was dazzling, but I was too tense to return it.

"Actually, I was thinking of maybe bringing in some films, reading a book together aloud, and . . . doing some compositions."

A howl severed my words as the aide slammed her finger in a file drawer.

### THE COMBISISHUN PROGRAM

I think that there is some techers think thare shit duos nod stink. Thes techers have som pouer and they bush it to much. The foning home bit can mak sum boeple mad, my old man get mad and give me shit. I hate sbeshal edjchykashon. I hate it when you ask when your'e going to get oud and they say vary soon and your'e still in. I been in eat years. Now she wonts us to right sunthing; owr

obinuon on the new timedable. My obinuon is I have'n
even started and all redy it make me puke.
Randy


Randy was banging his boot against the table's iron leg. "I enjoyed talking to your dad yesterday," I shouted over the din. This time my tele-
phoning had netted a parent rather than a brother. I'd seized the
opportunity to describe his son's erratic behaviour.

"Yeah, I know," Randy muttered sarcastically to the table top. Since
I'd last looked, a new swastika had appeared in the right corner. But to
these kids it was just lines, something rebellious, an insignia that heavy
metal groups used. Or was it?

I forced a smile. "You mad at me?"

Silence.

Ten minutes later he signalled. "Can I talk to yah?"

To talk problems through instead of brawling or cursing: that was a
skill I wanted them to learn. Hope perked as I followed him into the conference room.

He'd still rather be high, judging by the button on the jacket, but his
nails were clean and his hair washed, signs of the phone call's success.
"You know there's a policy of calling parents when a student's absent a
lot," I began defensively.

"Yeah, but yah told my dad I'm on drugs." He looked hurt.

I felt my cheeks burn. These conflicts of loyalty. Was I sworn to secre-
cy like a psychiatrist with his patient? I'd had the same dilemma over
Dori's suicide note. "I told him I thought you *might* be on drugs."

He gouged a pencil into the underside of the table.

"You never came right out and told me. What I said to him was that
sometimes, when you're moving around, and throwing things. . . ."
Embarrassed, I looked away.

"My dad said you said I was weird."

"I did not! I said your behaviour was sometimes . . . inappropriate."

For the first time he raised his eyes. "He asked if I took drugs. I told
him no." His mouth pulled back in a grin; under his hair the marijuana-
leaf earring flashed.

I looked at his crooked yellow smile. The two front teeth leaned against each other as if they were stoned. "Listen, Randy." How should I say this? "I'm a teacher, but I'm a parent, too, and if I thought one of my kids . . ."

". . . was on drugs you'd wanna be told," he finished.

I tried again. "Randy, I care if you're on drugs here. How can you learn if you're high? But outside school it's none of my business. You're twenty years old, for heaven's sake!" I stopped, pleased with myself. It sounded reasonable; it helped justify my betrayal.

He leaned towards me, surprisingly friendly. The talk had been a success!

"Can I borrow ten bucks?"

I leaned back. "What?"

"I need it for the spaghetti-eating contest; they're raisin' money for the United Way. Good cause," he added.

"Ten dollars. That's a lot of money. Will you pay me back?"

"Sure."

"When?"

"Thursday."

"What if you don't come Thursday?"

"Come on," he wheedled. "Yer such a nice teacher, and it's goin' to help the poor and the needy."

Trust. The burden of Dori's trust had frightened me. But being trustor, rather than trustee – that shouldn't be as hard. Maybe it would be good for Randy to have someone show him trust. Maybe it would teach him responsibility.

I reached for a sheet of paper. "Write an IOU – say when you're going to pay me back." I looked firmly into his eyes. "And sign it!"

"By the way," I added, the transaction complete. "Your dad mentioned he gave you twenty dollars for a school trip today. Where are you going?"

"Trip?" he said blankly.


Did Randy's father really know his son? I had an idea for an assignment. Why not ask the junior English class to write a letter to their parents (a letter *is* a paragraph, Colin), introducing the secret self, the real self. The letter they would never dare send.

Dear Mom,
Sorry to say the Real Me is gonna be a shock. I'm a real drinker. Almost every weekend I'm drinking with my friends. Most of the time it's maybe 10-15 beers. On the ocasion we drink real hard stuff like rye whisky, scotch and rum. I drink to get drunk I enjoy it quite a bit. Sometimes we go for a drive up and down the streets 95–100 MPH racing other cars. Yet it concerns me that I can let it get control of my life. Even as I write this letter I'm under the influence of ALCOHOLE.

David

■■

Dear mother I am sitting down tring to find away of riting you. This is hard for me. I feel we should be together and talk, not fight just talk For I feel you exspect to much of me. Not that I exspect to be waited on hand and foot it,s just well you know, friends.

Kevin

■■

Dear mom and dad,
You think Im getting along okay at the shelter, but Im not! I lie in bed at night and I can't sleep from worrying about whats goin to happen to us. I know your tryin to get us our own place again but when do you think thatll be? I can't take it any more!

Christie

■■

Dear Mom,
i wish you wuld let me do Anything like go Down Town and stay out Late. i hate comeing in telling you Where i'm at and Who with and What i'm doing like its a third degree Lecher!

Cammy

■■

Dear Mom & dad

Nothings fair anymore. You expect me to watch my brother 24 hours a day but yet you let Philip do anything he want's to he doesnt do any house work you said he has to take out the small white garbage yet you tell me to take out the big green garbage but you always put the small white garbage into the big green. You treat me like garbage.

Bill

■ ■ ■

### GOOD-BYE NOTE

Dear mom.

#1. It's not my fault your jealous and have all those hateful feelings towards my boyfriend but I been with him now for almost two years and I'm not giving him up for you

#2. You and Cathy seem to have a fantastic time together. And have stuck to each other like glue obviously you's don't need me

#3. At last but not least I tried you tried, we all tried and we just can't compromise so I think the best thing to do is go away and be happy and find my love.

Good-bye

XO

■ ■ ■

Ok dad I can't always say the things I want to say, so Fuck you you shit hole, you took off, you never payd no suport I hate your guts and I always will, If I ever see you I'll kick the living shit out of you, rob you, then kill you!

■ ■ ■

MISS SLONEKI

I DO NOT BELIEVE IN THE THINGS YOU LIKE USE TO
WRITE YOU SORT OF GET TO PERSONAL AND YOU LIKE
USE TO BE OPEN WITH YOU AND SOME OF USE LIKE ME
CANT GET OPEN WITH A TEACHER ITS LIKE PULLING

DOWN YOUR PANTS IN FROUNT OF THE CLASS. IF YOU
WOULD PULL UP YOUR DRESS IN FROUNT OF THE CLASS
THAT IS IMBARASING FOR YOU AND THE CLASS AND ME.
ANOMINUS

I shuffled the letters, put them in a folder, then stared after them into the open briefcase. Had I the right to have given such an assignment? To read confessions that their own parents were denied? And what should be expected of me? Was I required to reveal *myself*?

"D'you know Randy Edwards?" I asked Mr. VanBuren, the carpentry teacher. I was worried about the ten-dollar loan.

"Yeah, I had him last year in woodworking. Some kids were helping me weekends with a contracting job, and I offered him work. He didn't show." He frowned. "Yesterday one of my kids bought a calculator off him for ten dollars. It's worth about a hundred."

Ten dollars? My mind was working. "Well, what's the problem with this calculator?" It was obvious he was selling it to repay my debt.

"Hot property. Randy's on probation. Now he and Kevin Smythe are involved in this new business. They've been selling stolen items out of someone's garage. And not just calculators, either. This time he could go to jail."

"Kevin Smythe," I echoed bleakly, and sank into a chair. Partners. And it was I, standing in front of my jammed door, who had brought them together. And now Randy was breaking probation to sell "hot" goods for me.

"That ten dollars is to pay me back," I confessed to the priestly blue eyes, the white-haired halo. Mr. VanBuren's efforts on behalf of these kids extended far beyond anything that could reasonably be expected of him. For a moment I felt he might give me absolution, too.

"Randy Edwards owes you money?" Colin Beatty lifted his head from a book. "He owes me fourteen dollars."

"He owes me eight," said another, momentarily distracted from a crossword puzzle.

"I loaned him a calculator last year." The aide raised her eyes sharply from her knitting. "That's *our* calculator!"

"No, no, this one gives a printout," I said guiltily. It was the most she'd said to me in quite a while.

Nick Sawchuk put down the sports section. "Randy Edwards? He's the only guy I ever kicked off the cross-country team for cheating."

Everyone turned. "How?" I asked.

"Short cuts."

"Why'd you give him ten dollars?" Mr. Pritchett's contempt came from the corner where people played bridge.

"He needed the money for the spaghetti-eating contest. During United Way Week," I said weakly.

"That's only fifty cents!" Mr. Pritchett sniffed.

22

## PRITCHETT QUOTES DICKENS

From the Composition Program:

> ASSIGNMENT: "It was a large cellar, cold, dark, and damp. I couldn't hear any movement upstairs."
>
> Write a paragraph using the above sentences as your opening lines.

> It was a large seler, colt, dark, damb. I coulde'n hear
> eney moovment up stars so I snuck ub and seen a VCR on
> dob of the tv. I starded to unhook the wiers and Kevin
> come runin in and sed there home! so i finisht to unhook
> the wiers and graped the VCR we run oud the bak door.
> We sold it for $3.0000 and then we went partynging.
>
> Randy

I turned off my nose like a tap, took a quick breath in through my mouth, then determinedly ushered Peter into the small conference room. Thrusting his teachers' evaluation sheets towards him, I pointed out that every one of them remarked on his too-frequent absences.

"This is bullshit!" he retorted. "Am I failin' or not? I want to know now so's I can quit and go to work full time!" Red spotted his neck like an attack of measles.

"So quit!" Why was I saying that? "And when you're ready to work here, *then* you come back!" Why was I shouting?

His voice suddenly dropped. "Only thing is, I can't quit, or my mom won't get no Mother's Allowance."

"Then you'd better start coming to class! Where are your doctor's notes for all your absences?"

"Doctors?" he was yelling again. "They're bullshit! You go to 'em and they tell you you're sick! You already know you're sick or you wouldn't go to 'em!"

"Peter!" My head was throbbing. Why were my frustrations pressing in on me like these dark days of winter? Hadn't I had my share of successes lately? Hadn't I achieved some small gains with Ray? Wasn't the junior English class coming along nicely?

I leaned against the door and stared into his mushroom-white face. I wanted to shake him. With difficulty I kept my hands at my sides. "Why are you away so much?"

He looked around furtively. "My sister's got cysts on her ovaries. And my aunt died." He reached into his wallet and brought out a carefully folded obituary. "She died from the same thing my mother has – diabetes, asthma, and ulcers. But at least she got her last wish." My eyebrows rose, my anger slipping down this well of family woe. "See, she always wanted to be a Catholic. Before the operation they brought in a priest, and she was baptised. At least she's definitely in heaven, cuz she was paralysed right after, so she couldn't sin no more." I followed his mournful gaze to the ceiling, half-expecting to see his now beatified aunt.

"And now my cousins are livin' with us. They got three kids, miss. The baby cried all night. I wanted to punch its head in!"

"Peter." I shook my head to extricate myself from his life, this net that was falling over me. "I know it's hard at home, but you'll be leaving school this June! What are you going to do, with these kinds of habits? How will you keep a job?" It was so simple, why didn't he understand? And then, out of my frustration, I said it: "Do you want to be on welfare?"

He looked around wildly. "Ha!" he brayed to the wall, to the ceiling, to his finally happy aunt. "Once a welfare case, always a welfare case!"


The documentary was called *Gail Is Dead*. It traced the life of a young English girl from her promising early childhood through the institutions that followed: an orphanage, foster homes, special schools, a Borstal school, and, finally, the adult prison where she first tried heroin. At nineteen she was dead of an overdose.

Why did I choose this film to show to the kids in Special Ed? Because it was about a life that no one could turn around. It was a despairing thought, but one I was having more and more: there were certain people who couldn't, or wouldn't, stop the downward spiral of their lives.

"You won't change anything," Colin Beatty had warned and Pritchett had echoed. And now a student had said it, for wasn't that what Peter meant?

"You can write anything that comes into your head," I said, when the film was over.

Randy snickered. "Hey, Peter, why don't yah write about something yah know? Like jerkin' off!"

But Peter's head lay forlornly on the table. I felt a stab of guilt. Had the film made him fearful about his own downward spiral?

I bent over his still form. "Peter," I whispered, "if you're upset, one good way to help yourself is to write about it." I was doing that, writing almost daily in my journal. "Peter, write about what your thoughts are, right now."

At last his head stirred. In slow motion he sat up and reached for a pencil.

### THE GROUP HOME

About three or four years ago, I was in a group home. The house was realy nice, it had a pool room and a tv room, but it was in the middle of nowhere. The closes store was a twenty minute walk. Their was four of us and two home leaders. The four of us went to two a room. The fire exit was right at the head of my bed. Many of times I thought of runing away but that realy wouldn't work so good because I would get caught and besides at least I had food and warmth and also I would prolong my time. I realy don't know if it was that or I just could not get up the curage.

But the one thing I miss a lot is sitting at my window and watching the snow fall in the not dark but not light cold sky and seeing untouched snow over a huge field, and the snow will never be crushed because no one walks there.

"Peter?" He raised his face. And for a moment I could see, as if a fog had suddenly lifted, the contours of his jaw, the clear irises, the pupils. And suddenly I wanted to hug him, thank him, sing it out – to the other students, to the doubting aide, to Colin Beatty and Mr. Pritchett and the principal – to holler over the PA:

"Peter, what you wrote – it's beautiful!"

"I must say, the kids' writing gives me an extraordinary view into their lives," I said, looking around the table. "Their journals are incredibly honest, and their poetry and plays. . . ."

Mr. Pritchett's distaste transferred from Today's Hot Entrée, the shepherd's pie, to me. "Ah, yes, I've seen some of the things your students write." He glanced across at Colin Beatty. "And why would you want to know about their mean little lives, anyway?" Colin leaned forward, a hint of mischief gleaming in his eyes. Hilda Becker coughed uncomfortably.

"Well, I don't agree with *that!*" I said. "Who's to say one life is more worthy of being chronicled than another?" The forcefulness of my defence caught me by surprise. "And what exactly *is* writing if not self-expression, a means of communicating who you are! Anyway" – my blood was warming to this challenge – "I happen to feel it's good for these kids to write about personal experiences. It gives them the opportunity to understand themselves better, maybe, even, make changes. . . ."

"Colin tells me you've, ah, digressed from the course of study. Perhaps you haven't fully considered our students' futures. Ask yourself whether a plumber, a hairdresser, or a jailbird" – he gave a snort – "needs to learn to write poetry." He winked at Colin. Beside me, Hilda Becker squirmed.

He put down his cup. "I carry something around that you might find interesting, given your respect for great writers." Smirking, he reached into his billfold and extracted a piece of paper. "This is an excerpt from *David Copperfield.*"

> ". . . That sort of people. Are they really animals and clods, and beings of another order?. . . ."
>
> "Why, there's a pretty wide separation between them and us," said Steerforth, with indifference. "They are not expected to be as sensitive as we are. Their delicacy is not as shocked, or hurt very easily. . . . they have not very fine

natures, and they may be thankful that, like their coarse rough skins, they are not easily wounded. . . ."

"I'm familiar with that novel," I said. "Are you?"

Mr. Pritchett shifted. "Well, no, I'm a geography teacher, I don't really have time for nineteenth century English authors. I just happened to come across—"

"But Dickens himself came from a poor family. His father was in debtors' prison. He left school at fourteen and worked in a shoe-polish factory. His novels aren't an apology for the class system at all, they're an attack on it! David Copperfield is an abused child who struggles to rise above the contempt of certain people."

I found Hilda Becker staring, Colin Beatty's face twisted into a tight smile. Mr. Pritchett – who, it suddenly occurred to me, was very like a character from a Dickens novel, one of those small-minded clerks – was hastily paying his bill.

"By the way," I called to his retreating back, "our students *do* easily wound!"

■

From the Composition Program:

### SOMETIMES

Sometimes I am so confused I just want to stop time and rest, and when I am redy to get going again I just push a buton. But life does not work like that. (oh I wish it did) Life often feels like a vise you know like, you have to watch it at all times or Bang it squeezes you. Although I know I am only 18 you may think how can he be troubled, but every one has the wieght of problems. We just have to be strong. They say time heals all wounds, but let us not forget it still leaves scars.

Peter

23

# THE FAVORIT TEACHER

From a distance I could see that something had been written in the salt and dirt that caked my car. Had someone pressed hateful words into its vulnerable metal skin? I braced myself.

First I made out my name, then the rest: "I LOVE SOLNUKI – SHE A BABE."

A feeling of relief flooded me. Like this early March day with its damp south wind carrying the smell of spring, the message wasn't hate after all, but love.

"Look!" I chuckled to Mr. Pritchett as he climbed into his immaculate white Saab. "A belated Valentine's Day card."

He squinted at my unwashed station wagon. "The board does not cover damage to vehicles in the parking lot."

As the edge of my door swung out, Pritchett scowled from behind the steering wheel: "Watch my car!" But I didn't care – I had just been presented with a unique love letter.

I took in the smart jersey, the pleated pants, the new Nike Airs. "Leroy, you've not been in home-room for week and weeks! We've missed you! Where've you been?"

He loped, long-legged, to the window. "Ah, keepin' busy."

"Thought you was gonna get a job," Jamie said petulantly, between gulps of Coke.

"Soon, soon. But someone stole my ring. Can't quit school without my ring." He watched the students walking the melting snow path between the pines to the front door.

"How did someone steal it?"

"Just like this." He pulled on his finger.

"You let them do that?"

"Damn right! Don't plan to look down the end of a thirty-eight. That's right!" he nodded. "This dude carries a gun!"

"In this school?!"

"Better believe it! And I ain't gonna rat on no kid for no four-hundred-dollar ring. My life's worth more 'n that!"

"Someone carries a gun in this school?" I repeated, stunned.

"Me not sayin' notin'! The man's gonna lick two blood clot shots in mi head, star!" In his excitement Leroy had slid into his native Jamaican patois.

The word "pimp" rose above the whispering heads of Gus, Jamie, and John. "*Pimp?*" I repeated, loudly.

"That guy's nuts!" Gus burst out. "He was buggin' Dori to work for him." Dori. . . . The name made me sad. She'd been gone for a while.

Suddenly the bell rang. A space cleared around the door. A boy waited there like a shadow. The class tensed. Leroy froze. Then the shadow slipped away.

"Leroy?" I stopped at the door of the vice-principal's office. Mr. Taggert had been pulling on his hair again: it coiled as if a current of electricity had sizzled through each red wire.

"That's what the police are here for." He motioned out the window to the cruiser in the back driveway.

"His ring?"

"Yeah. A kid in the adjustment class took it. He gave it back."

"Leroy says the boy's dangerous."

"Yes. He's been in jail – for theft, assault. . . ."

"Does he really carry a gun?"

Mr. Taggert raised his red eyes to the two smiling boys on the wall. "The police searched his locker, didn't find anything."

I sat down heavily. "Are there *really* kids in this school who carry guns?"

He opened a desk drawer. It was crammed with lethal-looking knives of various lengths, brutal brass knuckles, metal balls bristling with spikes. In the back corner lay three guns.

To my horror he handed me one of them. "It's a replica. The others are pellet guns," he said, seeing my reaction. I touched the cold, shiny, blue-black barrel. Gingerly, I pushed it back. "This is what we've confiscated so far. We've never actually found a real gun. But you hear rumours. And our kids do have access. Some hunt, some are in the army. And it's not too hard to buy a gun on the street." He sighed. "It hasn't happened yet. When it does, I don't know what I'll do. . . ." His lips tightened.

"Do you think Leroy's in danger?"

"I think the police did a good job of warning the kid. Anyway, Leroy's a great runner, best on the track team, and he asked for a fifteen-minute head start before the police let the other guy go."

He smiled, and I smiled too; but against my ribs my heart was thumping: Gun-gun, gun-gun, gun-gun.


Distant voices, everyone hurrying to leave for the weekend. But I was anxious to finish my marking.

I heard a rustle. A beige envelope skidded under the classroom door. I got up and looked out. But the postman had disappeared. The halls stretched in both directions, empty.

"SOLNUKI": the printed letters on the envelope nudged me, but I couldn't quite place them. I opened the flap and pulled out a single white sheet.

### THE FAVORIT TEACHER

I know a teacher
unlike all the others.
This one is speshul
This one is smart
This one is wity atractive and cheery.
She can make a long day bearible,
a bad day good.
Older, yet young in her ways,

> easy to relate to, and so understanding,
> I sit in the classroom for eighty minutes a day,
> too long to be with som teachers,
> not long enugh with her.
> Miss Solnuki, as a teacher I am glad to know her.
> As a woman I would like to know her.

How lovely it was, how flattering! Just that line at the end made me uneasy. But surely the poet didn't mean "know" in the original, carnal sense. It was meant innocuously, of course, and it really was very sweet – but who could have sent it? Who had waited until I was alone, then slipped it softly, secretly towards me?

Dino, maybe. I pictured his smile framed in springy black curls. Sometimes he stayed after class to walk me down the hall. Then it must also be Dino who had left that message on my car.

There was nothing unusual in a student's having a crush on a teacher. But I would have to find a way to say something delicate, but firm, to discourage him.

Hilda was sweeping icing sugar off her desk when I came into the English office. Ego won over discretion. I showed her the poem.

Her mouth pursed. "I'd be careful," she said. "You really should go to Guidance and discuss it with them."

"Dino's a sweet kid. I'm not the least bit worried."

"You never know what's going on in his mind. He could attack you one day, kiss you, or worse!" She crossed her arms over her bosom protectively. Flesh pale as baloney peeked between buttons.

"Really, Hilda!"

"Well, I know about a situation in my last school. . . ."

He was hanging back at the table after the others had gone, and it seemed like the perfect opportunity. Silently I went over the words I had rehearsed.

"Dino, I've been wanting to talk to you." He smiled his glistening smile. "That writing on my car was really cute." He stared. "And that poem you wrote was beautiful – *very* beautiful. But. . . ."

A furrow punctuated his brow like a question mark.


But if Dino didn't write the poem, who did? Who was my secret admirer? I sat down at my cluttered desk in the English office, my eyes riveted to the envelope.

"SOLNUKI." A number of kids spelled my name that way. But the script, the press of it, as if energy had vented itself like escaping steam through the shaft of the pencil. There *was* someone who did that.

The poem itself was too neatly printed to be his, the spelling too good. But what if he had worked and reworked it?

Where had I put that other envelope he'd given me just before Christmas? Finally, in my bottom drawer under some old memos, I found it. "SOLNUKI." Same spelling. Same heaviness. Same shapes.

My hands trembled as I withdrew the picture of the two women on the beach; the naked one with dark hair.

What did he mean when he said "as a woman I would like to know her"?

The pounding in my head asked: What does Jack want?


I stayed late again, but this time I left the door open: with everyone gone, the halls were thick with a charged silence, as if listening for the creak of leather, the cry of a curse.

As I folded a test paper I sensed a presence. I looked up. Jack was standing in the doorway.

"Oh! You startled me!" He was wearing combat fatigues and a flak jacket. I'd never seen him dressed that way before.

"Where . . . where've you been? You haven't been to class for ages." I leaned back in the chair, trying to appear calm. The green uniform and black boots exuded a brutal power.

"I've been busy," he said softly. His eyes were pale moons floating in a white face. In outer space, I thought to myself. My eyes flew to the open door. The janitor would be somewhere on the first or second floor. Would he hear a scream?

"You know how you always want us to write things. Well, I been writin' lately. Some poems." I flinched. "And I made up a story. You're in it." His voice was toneless, his hair flickered, a flame at the end of a waxen candle. He came towards the desk, his heels thudding. His white fingers curled around an envelope, SOLNUKI written on it – that same way.

And suddenly I knew this story: damp-walled basement, musty mattress, rope, knife that springs, deadly as a cobra. "No!" I croaked, as if he'd already unleashed that knife. "I mean, it's getting late." I scooped up papers, coat, hurried past him. At the end of the hall I could see the janitor's cart.

Would I find Jack leaning against the hood of my car or crouched in the back seat? The parking lot was empty. The trees of the adjacent houses spread their bony arms against the grey, indifferent sky, but they couldn't reach out to help me if Jack came running, hollering his hunter's cries.

I got into the car, checked the back, then locked all the doors.

■

From a journal:

> Afew weeks ago was the worst Valentines day in my life. I woke up with the happy thought that I'm going to make my boyfriend (CLIFF) his favrit lemon pie, and I would take my sweet time to make that pie perfect.
>
> I ever so careful mesurd all the ingreedience, and made that pie so perfect that I could win a bake sale, and it took me four hours.
>
> Then around seven CLIFF (my boyfriend) came over, and so grumpy he sat down on the couch and picked up a magazine and started to read. I got realy mad, and grabed the magazine and, pulled him in the kitchen. I moved him infront of the pie that was siting on the table, and I yelled out surprise with such inthusiasem, and smiling I kissed him. He turned to me with a bord look, "I'm not hungrey" walk back in the living room, and started to read again. I

ran in to the living room grabed the magazine from his hand and through it across the room.

I sat down beside him camly and said "your not happy with me? are you"? then there was dead silence, "answur me god damit" then very quitly he said "no". "I think you better leave then". He got up walk to the door, and I followed. He put his jacket on, and his boots and I said "come hear", and he followed me to the kitchen. I picked up the pie I made with suck care, and through it hard in his face. "Happy Valentines Day".

24

■

# THEM

The teachers reluctantly waited out the introduction of the guest who'd been invited to the staff meeting, the tall, well-dressed, black superintendent of multiculturalism for one of the boards.

His talk began with a description of ethnic diversity: 40 per cent of all immigrants ended up in Metro. Visible minorities made up 15 to 20 per cent of Metro's population. There were seventy-five different racial and religious subgroups.

Scarborough was the fastest growing of the boroughs. In one month – September 1988 – three thousand immigrant children entered its school system.

The flicker of Mr. Taggert's hand, as it moved involuntarily to his head, caught my eye.

There was a tremendous need for teachers to understand the sensitivities of these immigrant children and their parents' fears. But the black student, he said, had a particular problem. Black parents were complaining that, under the streaming system, the schools were directing their children into basic-level courses. In a recent year more than 28 per cent of blacks were enrolled in basic-level courses, as compared to 4 per cent of Asians and 14 per cent of white children.

Nick Sawchuck whispered something he thought was funny into the autobody teacher's ear.

And what did those numbers mean? Recent provincial statistics showed that four out of every five basic-level students dropped out of school. That compared to 12 per cent of advanced students. Among racial groups, then, blacks were the most likely to leave school without a diploma. The stereotyping that assumed low expectations for blacks was conferring on them a life sentence of poverty and humiliation.

Several teachers were now looking at their watches.

He told his own story. When his niece and nephew came to Toronto from Trinidad, the Guidance Department put them back two years. Disgusted, he sent them home to Trinidad. Today, one was studying at Western, the other at the University of Toronto.

He, too, had experienced this stereotyping. When people asked him what he did and he answered, "Superintendent," their frequent response was: "Good for you!"

Nick Sawchuk caught up with me as I was leaving the library. "Bullshit!" he snapped. "Those kids from the islands bring it on themselves. I had one refuse to stand for the national anthem, said it wasn't his country. So I told him to go back where he came from!"

"What did you think of that speaker?"

Mr. Pritchett looked up suspiciously from his green jello.

"I mean, what do you think of this whole notion that black kids are being streamed into the special schools?"

"There's no racism here!" Nick Sawchuk's arm thunked down on the table like a hockey stick.

Hilda Becker sighed loudly and shifted in her chair. "I've had good kids, you know, collegiate-quality kids, black and white, and I've tried to steer them to a collegiate, and very few of them ever take the steps to . . . I just don't see where skin colour has anything. . . ." Her voice lost its way in her large chest, and she wandered back into the Black Forest cake.

Glumly Colin Beatty intoned: "Sooner let earth, air, sea, to chaos fall,/Men, monkeys, lap-dogs, parrots, perish all!"

"But what about the statistics?" I interrupted.

Mr. Pritchett laid his spoon carefully down. "Maybe those statistics are correct, but his *reasons* for them are wrong. The system doesn't put kids here; they *belong* here. Scarborough has a lot of Chinese – will some expert please come to this school and tell us why none of them are here?

Look around and you'll understand what's behind those statistics. Cultural expectations. Family expectations."

Family? Mr. Pritchett's father was an Episcopalian minister, I'd heard. But where was his son's compassion?

Nick Sawchuk had been waiting with barely contained glee. "What's long and hard on a black man?" he interjected.

"What?" Colin smirked.

"Grade three."


The mostly black audience sat excitedly in the cafetorium, waiting for the curtains to open. Rap was their music, and this concert was not to be missed. As anticipation mounted, folded programs skimmed the air like missiles; around the room good-natured scuffles erupted.

Suddenly, near the front, a tall black boy sprang to his feet. He stood out like the raised middle finger of a hand. "Hey, honky!" he yelled. He poked a long arm towards the far side of the cafetorium. "Honky," he taunted, "yah got a fuckin' ugly face!"

Everyone craned to see where the arm pointed. But none of the white kids in the far corner answered.

An angry restlessness had come over the audience, like wind that gusts through an open window. Now people were standing, moving, muttering. Fear brushed my skin, raised goose bumps on my arms. Against the far wall I saw Mr. Taggert turn, alerted.

The curtains parted; a rhythmic beat punched from huge speakers on the stage. Four black boys, their peaked caps perched sideways on high, flat-topped hair, their two-tone silk suits rippling, leaped out from the wings.

The audience fell back into the seats with a roar. Clap, clap, stamp, stamp – the beat enveloped the room. One performer executed back flips, another spun and jerked, as they lip-synced the rat-a-tat-tat. Across the stage boogied a brotherhood of black, athletic boys.

How amazing that the energy for hate and violence could turn so soon to dance and joy! I, myself, had failed to raise the lid of their prejudice, release the empathy that must be locked inside.

■

From a journal:

It happened last Friday night, this guy Duane I am
engaged to, we had a argument. I went to the dance, he
went to the bar.

After the dance I was walking to the bus stop with
friends. Duane pulled up he started to swear and make
Black jokes started to push and shove.

It all started as a joke bewteen them, then Duane started
in about blackes no good bastards saying things like hey
brother come on right now monkey man, then came the
crude remarks.

Soon the tempers showed people became hot headed
then rocks, feet and fists. As the night went on we had a
racial fight on our hands.

At the end of the night my arm was fractured, Rick had
his head cut open with a pop bottle, Duanes eye needed
eleven stitches in two places and he was charged with
imparied.

25

■

# WE SHALL OVERCOME

"A Family Affair." I raised my eyebrows to Sue, the quiet girl near the door, after I said the title. She nodded imperceptibly. That meant I was permitted to read the rest of her scene aloud. Since no one would publicize so private a matter, the nod also meant it was fiction.

> Chris: Richard called from the cop shop to say that Sherry was rushed to the hospital! She was doin the splits and she tore herself open!
> Me: My God! But why's he at the cop shop?
> Chris: They're accusin him of raping her.
> Me: Chris, don't bullshit!
> Chris: I'm not bullshittin! You better go to the cop shop, speak to him.
>
> (*I went to the police station*)
>
> Me: Can I speak to Richard S.? He was brought in today, he's charged with rape.
> Cop: I'm not the arrestin officer. Richard will be going to court tomorow, you can see him there.
>
> (*I started going histerical. My girlfriend and others grabed me and brought me outside.*)

Chris: Calm down, everything will be all right. Let's go find your mother.

(*At last we went back to my place, and mom was there. She was crying. I went up to her.*)

Me: What came over him? What would make him do something like that?
Mom: I don't know. (*crying*) I don't know.

(*A year has passed. He is in a treatment centre. He will not be going to jail. We used to have almost daily breakdowns, now only once a month. Everyone thinks rape is such a sin, but if it's a family member involved your thoughts change. No one in our family has any grudges about what has happened, because the person who did all this is our brother.*)

"Pervert!" Ray shouted, when I finished. His voice scattered the images of Jack that this shocking scene had called up in my mind. After a week checking the back seat of my car, I'd inquired yesterday at the office about Jack's absences. He'd quit, Mr. Taggert said. I'd gone straight to my desk drawer, taken out his poem, ripped it into tiny pieces. He wasn't supposed to enter my thoughts again.

This scene. . . . I forced myself to focus on positive things: a student creating vivid characters, a compelling situation. I snuck a discreet glance towards Sue, to see if Ray had hurt her feelings, but her expression betrayed nothing. "Not a pervert at all," I answered. "What's interesting is that the writer's managed, in this piece of fiction, to show that rapists are people too."

Sue lingered by the door when class was over, a quiet girl, easy to overlook. Now I noticed for the first time that she was rather pretty. A little overweight, and she was picking at the pimples on her chin when she came to the desk.

An awkward silence. "That was a very dramatic scene you made up, Sue," I said positively.

"I changed my brother's name 'cause some people here know him," she blurted. "He went to this school. And that girl he raped . . . she's my sister. I changed her name, too."

Something went dead inside my head, as if she'd kicked it.

"My sister had to have sixty or seventy stitches internally; she had stitches outside, too. She's young and real tiny. The other day she told me some of her stitches still ain't come out yet, and they're supposed to be all out by now. God, did we laugh!"

I couldn't stop staring at her. "How old was your brother when this happened?" I finally managed to say.

"Sixteen."

"Why . . . did he do it?" The numbness was moving down from my head, taking hold, like a dentist's freezing.

"I dunno. And you wanna hear something else? My mother took off with my two sisters when I was young, left me with my father and brothers. My stepmother beat me. I useta come to school black and blue." She laughed again, another joke I was missing.

"My father once unzipped me," she went on pleasantly, "in his sleep. We useta sleep on the couch together. I never told him in the mornin'." She smiled. Like an automaton I nodded again.

"D'yah wanna hear another problem?" She set herself down on the desk for the long haul. I got up, to give notice. "My father said as far as he's concerned all his kids're dead." She was an insistent blur, trailing after me. Why didn't she stop? "I haven't seen him for three years. My sisters say they hate him." I leaned against a locker to steady myself. "But I say you shouldn't hate yer own father, even if he done all those things." She shook her head and laughed: "Weird, eh? Weird, weird family!"

What Pandora's Box had I unlocked when I encouraged them to write about themselves? What did their mean, little lives have to do with me?


"The big problem in this school is Public Relations!"

Mr. Taggert's voice resonated from the head of the table. We were seated in the library at a meeting of the Liaison Committee, which I had joined when I was keen to bolster what the principal had implied was my precarious job. These days it was getting harder to be keen.

Mr. Taggert was proudly passing out his latest draft of a pamphlet he intended to distribute to the elementary schools. "I'd appreciate any other recommendations you might make," he beamed to the small group of staff, students, and parents.

Did Mr. Taggert really believe that this school's essential problem was its image? My sceptical eye moved down the page: "Sir Mackenzie Bowell offers students a positive educational opportunity . . . route to get back on track . . . warm and accommodating nature of the staff . . . productive careers and lives for our graduates." It rose to a crescendo: "The bottom line at Bowell is success!"

Lillian, the assistant head of Guidance, coughed politely. "I'm wondering if you're targeting the right people. Someone's got to stop the elementary teachers who are threatening from grade one that if a kid has trouble he'll end up here."

"Yeah, stop the teachers sayin' this school's for losers," a woman with dishevelled blond hair added.

"Word of mouth," Mr. Taggert was saying. "If enough people say enough positive things. . . ." He tapped the pamphlets piled in front of him.

"It's a good school," the president of the Student Council said.

"It's a excellent school!" a girl giggled.

"Some parents cause trouble," the woman with the messy hair continued, "tellin' their kids not to come here."

The thin woman across from me poked her short husband. He woke with a start. "We know some parents didn't want their kids to come here 'cause they hear there's so much drugs goin' around the school. And there's weapons, too!"

The vice-principal's hand moved towards his hair.

"Yeah!" the girl chimed in. "When the guidance counsellor said I should come here, *my* mother put me down."

"Word of mouth," Mr. Taggert repeated. He yanked several red strands.

"When I was at Hudson, I hated school! Now I love school!" The girl's head bobbed.

The lady across from me was solemn. "That's because the children were bruised and abused. The healing starts when they get here."

Reverential silence. The vice-principal's hand dropped gratefully.

"And other kids put you down, too." The vice-president of the Student Council was pimpled; his eyes swam behind thick glasses. "Like, when I'm with kids from a collegiate and they ask where I go, I say Bowell, but inside I don't really want to."

Finally I spoke up. "I've often wondered why this school chose such an unfortunate name." All eyes turned towards me.

"The proper pronunciation, you know, is *bōl*," the vice-principal said archly. It rhymes with—"

"Hole!" the president of the Student Council's whisper shot across the table.

The vice-principal coughed. "The Scarborough Board likes to give schools the names of prime ministers. It lends prestige and a sense of tradition. Sir Mackenzie Bowell was one of our earliest prime ministers – not a very important one, alas – but, well, all the others were taken."

"The kids make jokes about it," the vice-president protested.

"I don't think the name 'Bowell' is the problem," the blond lady said. "It's the words 'secondary school.' It sounds, yah know, second best. Couldn't it be called *technical* school?"

"A rose by any other name would smell as sweet," said Mr. VanBuren sweetly.

The vice-president snickered. "A bowel ain't no rose."

"That's just the sort of punning I'm talking about," I said.

"It's not the name, it's because we're ashamed," the blond lady confessed.

"Right!" the lady across from me seconded. "Sure there's doctors and lawyers, but there's tradesmen too! And believe me, they're just as important!" Her husband, now coming fully awake, snorted in agreement.

"I think it's" – the girl hesitated – "the reputation. When I first come here I was petrified. I heard all the rumours."

"Like it's a jail."

"Bars on the windows."

"If yah hang around with the wrong crowd you'll get yer head kicked in."

The vice-principal thumped the table. "There, in a nutshell, is our Public Relations job: to prove there's no substance to these rumours! Because anyone who comes here can see . . ."

". . . that a lot of people are afraid to go to the washroom," the president of the Student Council finished.

"Yeah," the vice-president added. "When I go I feel scared."

The woman across from me frowned. "Have you ever been accosted? Maybe it's just your imagina—"

"No it ain't! Four guys in black-leather jackets, doin' dope, pushin' you. . . ."

"They line up, twenty of 'em sometimes, watchin' you, throwin' pennies. I save it till I get home!"

"I been sprayed with fire extinguishers."

"Fires in the trash cans."

"Someone tryin' to sell you a stereo."

"A stereo!" all four parents cried in unison. Everyone's gaze zoomed in on the vice-principal.

"It's people from outside," he croaked, now raking his scalp. His hair was exploding like a small atomic cloud.

He began to collect the pamphlets. "It's hard to change a school's image. But if enough people. . . ."

From the junior English class:

> ASSIGNMENT: "Write a paragraph expressing your views on whether your school should change its name."

> i think it will be good for this school to Clean a slate. We should be able to say bowal with out other people snaring at us. They outamadicaly think you do Drugs and you Skip school and you Fail but there are sum people Who arn't like that Sum of the People just have a Leraning Disblity.
> > Cammy

■■■

> Sir Macensy Bowl shouldn,t have the name changed because our school has a good reputashun of being a ruff school. With a new name people would say "what

school is that"? and then you,ld feel like two cents.

Kevin

■ ■ ■

THE NAME SHOW THIS SCHOOL IS SHIT!!!

ANOMINOUS

■ ■ ■

This school is alot better then my old elmentery school, that place really sucked the bag cause if you skipped you otomaticly got caught cause every teacher knows every student and where they go after school and what they do before school. But in this school no one cares where I go or what I do, now thats great! So if the name gets changed that better not.

Bill

■ ■ ■

I know a place called the Metropoltan Toronto Family Resadence. But every person knows what it realy is. A fancy name don't fool any body. And it don't make it no more bearable.

Christie

A hole gaped in the front foyer's glass door. Broken edges sagged in, concentric circles radiated out. It was a cobweb spun by a spider gone berserk.

"Who did it?"

"That kid with the temper put his fist through it. David . . . David what's-his-name?"

"Dave Blane," Mr. Taggert said. He was standing outside my classroom door clutching his computer slips like a wilting bouquet. "He's kicked out. Got into a mêlée with some kids, broke someone's nose, then punched in a door." A shirt-tail lapped out of his pants, a sign he'd been summoned to stop the violence. "Completely, and I mean completely, out of control!"

"What was it over this time?"

"Something small."

"Do you happen to know if his mother went into the hospital? Because, you know, he gets very upset when she goes in. And she was due to go." He nodded sympathetically. "So how long is he out this time?"

"This is it, Jill," he said heavily. "I can't keep suspending someone indefinitely."

David, Dori, Dori, David. What was the point of investing in these kids?

His voice softened. "Jill, may I give you a piece of unasked-for advice? Something I've had to learn the hard way?" I nodded dumbly. "If you expect anything from these kids," – his voice climbed in momentary anger – "they'll break your heart!"

Forbidden words! They articulated something I hadn't quite been willing to admit: that one might come to love these kids; and for that they would hurt you. Did they explain Colin's rote lessons, Mr. Pritchett's cynicism? Why Hilda just showed movies? Like snails they lived in a shell, protecting the soft part.

Out of the bouquet he extracted a slip: "David Blane: deleted." That was the euphemism they used, like "passed away" for "dead."

David signalled from the corridor outside Special Education. "Got into a fight," he called, holding up a bandaged hand. He smiled crookedly through a swollen upper lip. I went out to him. His cheek was badly bruised, but the worst were his eyes, they kept ducking and darting, as if they were still in a fight. "I'm out," he said thickly, "but don't worry, I'll get my book in, I'll write the exam." His eyes leapt away to the wall.

"Make sure you do," I said, choking. These were the little lies one shared at partings, to make them easier. But he was gone for good now. And I hadn't turned him around. Hadn't made any difference, none at all.

I pressed his uninjured hand. "David, please look at me!"

His eyes stopped. "That's quite a grip," he slurred.

"David. Bye."

He grinned. "Bye . . . Mom."

He turned away; he pushed the glass door.

I marched abruptly back to my class. I would not watch the back of that small, frail boy disappearing down the hall.

Mr. Taggert rounded up the peas and the carrots with his fork, segregating them into two neat piles. "Spent the last three hours looking after crap," he muttered. "Can't seem to get to the important stuff."

"I saw all those kids in the office for detentions this morning," I said.

He sighed. "I don't think detentions do one bloody thing."

"I suppose they're token punishment."

"That's it – token." He stared glumly at his Salisbury steak. "I've been chasing kids, having conferences with parents. One woman this morning told me the kid's not living at home. I said, 'Where's he living?' She said, 'Oh, maybe with a Bruce, or somebody with a name like that.' I mean, she doesn't even know where her kid's living! Now we're getting our new kids for next year. There's one girl, fourteen years old. The report said she didn't know who at home she was related to. The counsellor's advice was: 'Choose the one you most like.'" He laughed incredulously. "Next year's batch has more problems than I've ever seen. I mean, they're so young."

This was not the lunchtime conversation I'd been hoping for, I was thinking resentfully.

"Did you know that kids from lower-income families are twenty-three times more likely to end up in basic level? That children from families on welfare are three times more likely to end up failing, or being sent to classes for slow learners?" He pushed the peas even farther into the corner, like banished children. "That only forty per cent of kids from working-class homes are in collegiates, compared to eighty-eight per cent of kids from middle-class homes? Did you know that employers favour collegiate dropouts over graduates from special schools? Did you know . . . ?"

Having lost faith in Public Relations, Mr. Taggert had now converted to Depressing Realism. "Please," I silently pleaded, "enough!"

His head tipped into his hands as if it had been severed. "I mean," – his voice leaked out from between his fingers – "how are you going to help kids like this?"

It had taken much, much longer than I thought, but at last we had finished reading *The Contender* aloud in junior English class. Our hero, the Harlem kid, had overcome a demoralized neighbourhood and drugged-out, delinquent friends; through discipline and determination, he had become a skilled boxer.

But his manager didn't want him to fight the last match of his career. The man he'd been paired with was stronger; Alfred was outclassed. But Alfred insisted. He had been a failure all his life, and he needed one final event to prove to himself that he had the courage to change, to make his life better.

"Now you know, too," the manager said softly, after Alfred had persevered through the brutal battering. Though he lost, the crowd was on its feet, roaring approval. Of his heart.

My voice choking, I slowly closed the back cover, and laid the book gently down.

"Stupid book!"

"The end sucked!"

"Took us two fuckin' months to read!"

"Where's she find these books?"

"In the garbage, that's where."

"I'll collect 'em." Bill jumped up.

Why had I even bothered? They couldn't see themselves in this Harlem boy. Couldn't identify with his courageous pursuit of goals. These kids were hopeless. Even if there was a job for me at the end of this year, I'd refuse it. Why not go back to being a lady of leisure, well treated by sales staff and waiters, whose biggest worry was which ballet subscription series to select?

"I'd like you to think," I said desperately, "just think, for one minute: What did Alfred have to overcome?" No hands raised, half the books scooped up. I answered my own question. "He had to overcome poverty, drugs, the bad influence of his friends, prejudice." Now the books three-quarters gone. "Haven't some of you ever had something to overcome?" The books landed on the shelf with a final thud. "Like . . . say" – last chance, groping frantically – "prejudice?"

The word seemed to quiet them. Had I struck a chord?

"We're prejudiced against cuz we go to this school," Cammy offered timidly.

Sudden machine-gun agreement: "If I had a Bowell hat, I wouldn't wear it."

"If I had a jacket, I'd tear off the letters."

"I never tell people I go to Bowell!"

"I say Laurier!"

"Macdonald!"

"They say: 'You're a M.B. Boy, you must be dumb!'"

Their bodies were facing me now; heads nodded. "Then we all have something, don't we, our own, well, boxing match, our own goal, something we're fighting to overcome?"

In big letters across the blackboard I scrawled, "I SHALL OVERCOME!"

> The first day i found out about my Leraning disblities was in Grade six. mister hart called me down to his office. and Told me that i would have to gorto joseph Brant in the SLD class. i tryed Very hard their but i was Still in grade 6 level in 7 and 7 in 8. i am All ways goin to keep Tryng to Over Come my leraning Disblity.
>
> Cammy

∎∎∎

> I have a very bad problem with what we call *zitts* (pimples) I have tired everything! They just keep coming! I,ve went to see doctors but they don,t do nothing So Il,l just have to fight harder and overcome these unvited visitors!
>
> Kevin

∎∎∎

> I overcame my fear of death three years ago when my great grandmother died I thought that everyone would died my parents my sister even my brother that very same day. Until one night my parents came in my room and saw me cring they talked to me. Then I understood that when your time comes it just comes and you have to accept it or you do like I did be afraid of death itself.
>
> Nadine

■ ■ ■

We're still livin in the shelter but I am tryin to make the best of it any way. And my dad says soon their goin to find us are own place. Then he promised were goin to get a big white dog like we had a long time ago when we lived in the country.

Christie

■ ■ ■

I HATE DOIN ASS-INMENTS!! BUT MAYBE IF I OVERCOME THAT I COULD SIN MY NAME.

ANOMINUS

■ ■ ■

I will overcome about school. I wanted to quit but now I undersatnd not to becaus I need my educashun. If I did quit everyone in my family would be mad at me and I can't afford that becaus I want to stay home. I going to school untill grade 12 and get my diploma. Then I can get a job and not be a bomb on the street like some people I know.

■ ■ ■

My biggest dream is to Be a entertainer Because I enjoy making people laught. I am getting to apoint where people just look at me and laught. One person look at me and said, is that my real face or was I just trying to be funny.

I live with my family of six and all my life it seem like I haven't really accomplish nothing much and all my brothers has, so mother constantly remine me of this. I've one brother name Nigel everyone in the family adore Him and my mother always talking things like why can't you be like Nigel? So I said it can't be my fault because if god wanted me to be like Nigel He would've made us twin.

But one thing I got is creativity and since my life doesn't seem like it's meanfully I entend to joke about it alot. Since I failed at every other thing I hope this dream will come true.

P.S. Comb your hair during a blizzard. Only youll know the difference.
P.S.S. That a example of my humer.


Clive sat until the last person had left, then came to my desk. Repeatedly he ran his fingers along the fold of his sheet of paper, until it was razor sharp. "I want to overcome this school!" exploded out of him. "I want to go to a collegiate!"

I rested my hand on the compositions. To keep the contact. Because I had already glanced at them. Through my fingertips I could feel the heat rising from the pencil lead, warmth I wanted to retain during the coming spring break. I'd never seen them write as ardently.

"Why are you so set on a collegiate?"

"Cuz the people who graduate from here get dead-end jobs."

"Well, maybe they don't get the *best*. . . . Anyway, I think you could make it in a collegiate. You've got the ability." He looked back doubtfully.

At the door he turned, a small dark figure. "D'you have something to overcome, too, miss?"

The question caught me by surprise: sudden tears pricked my eyes. I felt myself nodding. Our eyes met, and his face bloomed into a smile. Then he ducked out and disappeared.

As I stared at the smile hanging in the empty place below the lintel, I began to hum that song. I hadn't heard it since my university days, when I'd marched for civil rights, for equality, for hope.

By the time I'd packed my papers it was pealing like a bell.

Deep in my heart,
I do believe,
We shall overcome some day.

26

SPRING

Everything was on the move: water rushing down the gutter in front of my house like a spring freshet; a flock of Canada geese above Morningside Avenue, black scissor blades shearing winter's ties; and crows descending to the pines, as if a gang of kids in black-leather jackets had hunkered down.

As I started up the front stairs of the school I watched the window-washer on the ladder. He was scrubbing the glass, trying to make it clear and new. But hard as he rubbed, some of those stains were resistant.

I paused outside home-room. Down the hall I could see the wink of John's pink midriff as he leaned against a locker, talking to Gus. Beside them, Jamie was swigging a soft drink. Dori was gone, Leroy hardly came. But the first morning after spring break, I was determined to fight off the bleakness.

The sound of glass shattering jolted me. I glimpsed a kid running down the hall, out the exit to the driveway.

Air – stale, stagnant – rushed out through the hole, fleeing after the boy. But now new air could come in, too. Green promises were stealing down the corridor; teachers turned, students lifted their heads, sniffing the fresh, the fragrant. . . .

I recognized the voice immediately. "Dori! It's been so long! How've you been?" I visualized her at the other end of the line: peroxided curls, bright blue eyes, sassy butt.

"I'm at home. I was in the hospital," said the muffled voice.

I sat down at the telephone table, readying myself. Something bad had happened: that was Dori's way.

"Neil called on Friday at two in the morning cryin' his head off, said he was goin' to kill himself. I went hysterical. Brad took me over." She was back with Brad? "By the time I got out of there, he had to take me straight to the hospital."

Those bruises – I'd been right! "Dori, I hope you're finished with Neil!"

"He hit me before." Her voice seemed swathed in bandages. "Swore he'd never do it again. He . . . takes fits sometimes. My mom told me not to see him when he gets like that." Only then . . . ? "Anyways, I called cuz I wanted to wish yah happy birthday. I had the card all ready."

"Oh, Dori!" In the middle of her crisis this girl in tight jeans and bandages had thought of me. A little girl whose boy-friend beat her up – would beat her up again – had thought of me on my worst birthday.

My crisis, too, this birthday that forced me to stop, look in the mirror, see things I didn't want to see: a forty-year-old girl, still unsure, unfinished. Some distance behind her, a skull gaped back.

A light tap on the door. To my surprise, Dori stepped shyly in.

Past the staring Kevin, the whispering Christie, she walked across the front of the room, hugging the white rabbit-fur jacket to her body. She handed me an envelope.

"What's the matter with your hand?" I whispered the question, trying unsuccessfully to keep private this longed-for meeting. In front of us, eyes probed.

She held up her bandaged wrist. "Fracture."

I pointed to the Band-aids across her forehead, above her purple eye. At least he'd left the rest of her beautiful face alone. "Stitches," she said. She smiled. And suddenly I knew she was proud of those wounds, emblems of Neil's love, as much as a ring or a gold heart.

I opened the envelope and pulled out a card. On the outside she'd written, "To the Best Teacher Ever." On the inside, at the bottom, she'd drawn hugs and kisses – hugs and kisses that I ought to return, if I didn't feel so watched, so awkward, so like a teacher. Because when would I see her again? And what state would she be in?

Hesistantly, I touched her cheek.


Morosely, Peter stared into space. Randy's eraser bits sailed by his head and he didn't even duck. "What's the matter? You don't look well."

"It's a lot of things," he muttered.

"Like what?"

"Walkin' home yesterday," he gritted his teeth, "fuckin' nigger come up to me, asked me for a smoke."

"Not 'nigger,' 'black.'"

"I told him I don't got any. He searched me, took the whole deck! Fuckin' *nigger*! You just can't get ahead. You try and try, then just when you think you're goin' somewhere, somethin' pushes you down."

"You're going somewhere, Peter!" Behind us the aide, tending to Dino's work, nodded in agreement.

"Haw, haw!" he brayed bitterly. "Once a welfare case, always a welfare case."

"Lots of poor people have made a better life for themselves!" I said urgently. Had I caused this discouragement by bringing up the subject of welfare during a previous conversation? "You've got ambition and determination!"

"But I'll haveta look after my mother."

"You'll get a job!"

"It's harder, though. And my mother, I think she's sick again. No one sleeps twenty-four hours a day unless they're sick." I had a flash of the mother I'd never met, an older version of dirty hair and smell, horizontal on a sofa. "And my father. . . . I got along without him for thirteen years, and it never bothered me. But today I could kill him!" He looked around wildly. "Fuckin' nigger! I'm gonna take self-defence. Next time I see him, I'm gonna make sure he gives me a carton! No, I'm gonna break his leg! Both his legs! Actually," – his voice fell to a whisper – "I can't hurt no one."

He hung his head.

■

From a journal:

> There is so many changes that I would like to make in
> my life. Sometimes I wish I could just forget everythin that
> upset me, but so many things has fallen apart. It's not only
> the falling apart it's the putting back together. The pieces
> never seem to fit just the way I remember. My life was
> always so simple, and a risk was never taken, now my life is
> full of them and my spirit shaken. Changes in life
> is something I will have to get used to. But I can live
> through it because all of us have to change.
>
> Christie

# 27

# SLEEPING BEAUTY

"As you know, too many students are staying after school unsupervised," Mr. Taggert said, addressing the staff. "The potential for vandalism and theft is obvious."

"Why is it they won't come during school, but after school they won't leave?" the autobody teacher asked.

Several proposals followed. Mr. Pritchett suggested that a police cruiser park outside the school every day at dismissal, but that was voted down as excessively forceful. Mr. VanBuren suggested that a core of staff stay late to round up kids, but that was voted down as excessively inconvenient. Then Mr. Taggert suggested music. All eyes turned on him questioningly. "Classical music," he said.

At 3:00 the bell rang; at 3:01 Operation Sleeping Beauty went into effect. Up and down the corridors, through the crowded foyer billowed Tchaikowsky, a cloud of poison gas. The students milled about, confused; then they ran for the door. Masses of them poured out the exits.

At 3:15 there was no one left in the halls.

I took a chair from the English office and propped it against the wall near the glass doors – an ideal position for a border guard. I could control the passage of kids and have a rest, all at the same time. I settled across from the door to the boys' washroom, and watched shafts of pale sunlight slip along the floor.

The washroom door swung open, splintering the patch of light. Out came Jack. But what was he doing here? Hadn't he quit in February?

He was carrying something: what was it? This time it wasn't an envelope – it was long, metallic. A lead pipe.

He was coming straight at me, like a robot, no expression, just that pallid face and lank hair. Then, all of a sudden, he raised the pipe above his head.

I froze, forcing myself to sit still, silent, no sudden movement, bluffing him, acting as if he were bluffing me. For a moment I could hear the pipe whistling past my ears, feel its wind ruffling my hair before it crashed down on my skull.

He stopped just in front of me and lowered the pipe. "I wouldn't hurt you," he said. Still nothing in his face; the pale eyes blank. "Why would I hurt you? You're a nice teacher."

He turned, went down the hall, around the corner, back to plumbing class. Of course – sometimes the shop teachers gave pieces of hardware as hall passes.

I sat in my chair, not moving; and now I became aware of a pounding in my ears, like fists beating against a locked door.

When I found the telephone memo in my mail-box, my heart sank. What new bad thing had happened?

"Neil gave me a gold chain with my initial yesterday," Dori's voice resonated through the receiver. "He wants us to get engaged!"

I sat speechless while it dawned on me: to that bastard who beat her up? I had to do something! "How old are you, Dori?" I mumbled.

"Sixteen."

"That's awfully young! You have *lots* of time! Think of all the things to do out there in the world before you settle down!"

"My mom got married when she was sixteen. She wants me to. He wants me to."

Dori, he sent you to the hospital, he'll do it again! "But it shouldn't be what they want. It's what *you* want."

"I think" – I could hear her smile – "I'd like to."

I pressed the ear-piece against my temple to keep it from falling.

A letter never sent:

> My dear Dori,
>
> What was the secret behind your smile? You needn't tell me – it is every girl's: the prince, the kiss, the miraculous awakening.
>
> My dear sleeping beauty, marrying this man will not be the fairy tale you dream of. It will be a nightmare, then a rude awakening!
>
> When I was a girl I stood on the same threshold as you. But I never thought: Not *whom*, but *what* do I love? I never thought: What do I really want to do with my life?
>
> Today it's different, you can wake *yourself*. Today the threshold faces out. Don't you know that, Dori?
>
> Why don't the girls here know that?!
>
> With much affection and concern,
> Ms. Solnicki

"Is that you, Peter?" I said into the receiver.

Pause. "Yeah."

"It's Ms. Solnicki. Where have you been?"

"Takin' a shower."

No one who smelled like Peter took a shower! Still, that the excuse was in his head was a good sign. "Showers are good things, and of course everybody ought to take them. But you're supposed to take them first thing in the morning. We've been calling for the last couple of days."

"I been sleepin'. I hurt my knee."

"Peter, come to school! Would . . . should I pick you up tomorrow?" Why did I say that? A teacher wasn't expected to chauffeur reluctant students. Besides, I'd never been in one of their homes before.

A street number meant a house, trees, a lawn, didn't it? That must be why I drove three times past the drab, grey building rising between a used-car lot and a self-serve gas station.

At last I pulled into the driveway and parked near the garbage bins. A sign said "Metropolitan Toronto Housing." Two old men peered out through the grimy front window. A slim young woman in tight jeans pushed a stroller through the door, and I slipped in past her.

The sour odour of urine hung in the corridor. I held my breath. There was no knocker and no bell, so I rapped with my knuckles.

A puffy face peeked out. The door opened farther to reveal a wide woman stuffed into a frayed, pink, quilted bathrobe. "Come in," she said. "Peter's just gettin' ready." I stepped into a tiny living-room.

She motioned for me to sit down on the faded, flowered couch – perhaps the very bower where, according to Peter, she slept away so many hours. On the coffee-table sat a vase of red plastic roses. A TV faced us from a shelf cluttered with dogs and shepherdesses. On the wall hung a picture of the crucified Christ.

Her skin looked like crumpled paper. I stared at the grey and black bristles on her chin.

"There's this problem with Peter's attendance," I said, forcing my eyes to focus instead on the artificial bouquet. "Is there anything you could do to get him to school more often?"

"Well, I do my best, but it's hard bringin' up a child on yer own." Her smoker's voice was gravel. "You haveta be both father an' mother." She eyed the back room, then lowered her voice conspiratorially. "I wish I'da had him twenty years ago. My health ain't too good now and I don't got much money."

"I'm sure it's hard," I said. "I just wish his attendance. . . ." My finger drew concentric circles in the dust on the coffee-table.

"Oh, but he's sickly, yah know, gets headaches, and he's got asthma," she wheezed. "He useta be in a group home, on medication. But I took him off. He hasta learn to control hisself." Her forehead puckered. "Still, he's improved a lot. Don't know whether it's the school, or maybe it's me. . . ."

"You've done well!" I said suddenly. I wanted to smooth out all those creases.

At that moment Peter appeared, glancing from his mother to me with tight embarrassment.

She struggled to raise herself from the sagging couch. Finally she stood, her bosom heaving with the exertion. "What I always tell myself is . . . if life was a bowl o' cherries, yah wouldn't be able ta smell the roses."

28

■

# LETTERS TO THE COPS

The 401 had changed since the dark, winter afternoons when I had driven Christie to the shelter; from the height of the Don Valley Parkway the car swept down into green lacework, the bushes glowing on the grassy slopes, the Don River catching the sun, looking, from a distance, as if no detergents nudged its banks, no rainbow oil glistened.

Christie was telling me about her community of the homeless. "This lady's got three little kids, another on the way, and her husband, he don't. do nothin'. Only one day, he was takin' care of Casey. . . . You don't grab a eight-month-old kid by the pyjamas and throw him against the wall cuz he's cryin'!" I glanced at her angry profile. "I feel so sorry for her! That's why I baby-sit."

It was hard to remember the girl from the fall – green hair, or red, or flaming orange, like the leaves. In those days she went out of her way to make people miserable.

Now she was telling me about a boy who'd been admitted on the weekend. He'd run away from home, been kicked out of school, charged with passing stolen cheques. Already, everyone in the shelter was blaming him for things.

Last night he'd called her into his room to unburden himself. At the end of their talk he'd asked her to come nearer. Then he hugged her. "I just needed that," he said.

She was facing me, her eyes moist. Admiration welled up in me. Once Christie had been in need of shelter; now she was giving it.

Then, for one moment, with her dark eyes, her adversity, I saw Anne

Frank again. In the same book where I'd learned the word scabies, I first read about the selections. A survivor recounted that during a selection for the gas chambers, when each person had to walk naked before the SS doctor, Anne had encouraged her sister, Margot. Urged her to walk tall, as if she still had her health, still had courage. Even in those conditions Anne had not been crushed. Not yet.

"Anne gave shelter," I said, under my breath.


"You're supposed to be following the reading, Dino, and I can't see your eyes," the aide said. We were seated at a round table in the Special Ed area as Dino stared from behind his new, mirrored sunglasses.

Randy obliged by knocking them off.

Dino leaped to his feet. Chests puffed out, they faced each other in fury, a match touched to tinder.

"Don't touch me!"

"Eat shit, yah fuckin' wop!"

I jumped up and ran around the table. "Hey, guys. . . ."

"Suck cock!" Randy hurled over my head.

"Yah wish!" Dino answered, around my back.

"Stop it!" I was the buffer seated between them as reading resumed.

The bell was about to go when Dino went back to his desk. He fumbled among his papers. "Randy," he called out angrily, "you take my cigarettes?"

"You accusin' me of stealin' yer cigarettes? I didn't touch yer fuckin' cigarettes!" Randy swaggered over, cowboy-style. They eyed each other, chest to inflated chest. Suddenly Randy grabbed Dino's narrow black-leather necktie. He pulled on it, right up at the neck. Dino's face went red.

"Hey, guys. . . ." (God, couldn't I find anything else to say?)

Randy pulled, Dino pushed, and I rushed between them. Beneath grimace and rattle I pried, but their connection held firm. "Get the fuck outa my way!" Randy spat through his teeth. I pried with all my might.

"Now yah got me in shit. We'll be suspended!" Dino gasped, as Mr. Taggert huffed through the door, trailed by Nick Sawchuk.

I slumped in a chair and studied my shaking hand. Did it look somehow different? A reel of film ran backwards in my mind, stopped at that fight in the fall. I replayed my timid fluttering of six months ago. This time my hand had not run away.

My happiness found its voice in the birds singing in the pines, its face in the yellow light that late April poured through the window.

"Colin," I said. He lifted his dark head and the light scattered. "These plays are wonderful!"

"Even to the dregs and squeezings of the brain,/Strain out the last dull droppings of their sense," he muttered.

Why did he give out these strange quotes? "Colin," I said, as if I were shaking him, "can't you understand that writing plays can help these kids improve their English skills as much as writing paragraphs?" I drew out the one that gave me particular pleasure. Though still jousting from his desk in the back corner, Ray was at least completing enough assignments to pass. "Listen."

(*Around the dinner table.*)

Mother: Ok you guys come and get it.

(*Everyone sits down at table.*)

Father: Were's Ray?
Susan: He's at school daddy. I left him there with Kevin and Randy.
Father: Didn't I tell him not to hang around with those boys with their bad news.
Mother: Oh dear stop worrieing its . . .
Father: Were where you? Your late!
Ray: aamm me and some buddies where throwing a frisbee.
Mother: Call your sister and come to the table.
Ray: Cathy come for dinner!
Cathy: Coming.
Father: Why are your eyes red?

Ray: I don't know.

Susan: Were's my fox shirt Cathy?

Cathy: I don't have it.

Susan: Well, which one of your friends got it?

Cathy: Piss off!

Mother: Enough!

Father: that's right. now you young man, explain why your eyes are so red.

Ray: maybe there sore.

Father: I say you been smoke dope.

Ray: and if I was. (*Ray says it in a cold and harsh way*). Who the hell are you? To tell me what to do.

Father: i'm your father!

Ray: No your *their* father (*pointing at Cathy and Susan*) not mine, if you don't remember let me remind you your my stepfather a replacement for my real father, you mean nothing to me you got no fuckin authority over me!

(*Ray walks out of the house in a rage, with his mother screaming.*)

Mother: Your just like your old man! When your finished school you can get the hell out!

"Vulgar," Colin announced. A small smile slithered around his mouth.

"That is the stupidest—!" I sputtered. "That is an incredibly narrow view! Can't you see what he's caught here? Conflict! Character! Emotion! Real life! Isn't that what a writer *does*?"

The oily smirk spread.

"Colin, you've taught English here for years! How can it be you've never seen past their 'unclear, incorrect sentences' to the expressiveness in their writing, the humour, the insight, the God damn humanity?!"

"I think you're reaching, Jill."

"Just tell me," I cried, waving the play in a tight fist, "tell me once and for all why a paragraph, or a page of sentence exercises, or your precious overhead projector, is a better teaching tool than this!"

Across the wide expanse of two desks he looked at me, and he said nothing.


Out of the corner of my eye I spotted the distinctive gleam of a police car in the front driveway. That gave me an idea for the junior English class: letters to the police. And perhaps, I suggested, we might actually mail them.

> Dear Sir,
> I would like to know why you beat up young people when there drunk. What do you do with the beer and drugs you take off of them? Why don,t you admit it when you beat someone up? And why do you sware at young poeple? I was once in a police car with 2 police oficers and they said they like putting little shit,s like me in jail.
> Yours truely<br>Kevin X

■ ■ ■

> Dear Sir,
> I have seen some of your officers at the scarboro town center under the cover in the food court. you can tell that they are cops 5 miles away. 1) They all sit toget her. 2) There guns hang out of there coat. 3) Some carry small bags witch probly have cuffs, papers, ect. inside them. 4) They all have mustashes. 5) They wear funny brands of jeans.
> I think that if you plan on catching some of these asshole gang dudes, you gota clean up your act.
> Observer

■ ■ ■

> To Who This Might Concern (and I hope it'll)
> You should not judge people for their colour you should judge them by their actions if they comit a crime. Like if we were walking in a mall you tell us to leave or ask

us stupid questions. Some of us just want to walk in
a mall or on the street with out being hurrassed with
racialism.

Experienced.

■ ■ ■

I MYSELF HAVE HAD MY CONFLICTS WITH POLICE AND I
WAS BEATIN OVER THE HEAD WITH A PHONE BOOK WHICH
HAS RESALTED IN ME BEIN NEAR SIGHTED FOR THE REST
OF MY LIFE.

THANK YOU

ANOMINUS

■ ■ ■

Dear sirs,
I have had a bad experience with being charged by an
investigater who was interogatering me with his fists, but
that is because I had a record as long as his arm. After
stopping causing trouble when I reached 16 yrs you still
hastled me but its wore off now. Now I've used you for
when my car got vandalized and when we got a gang fight
on my front lawn. So its real nice to have you guys around
to keep the law in order, but I hope you could treat
teenagers accorded to each individual.

Reformed Teen

The letters had already been tucked into their envelopes when it
occurred to me that perhaps I should check with the principal before I
sent them.

Now, finally, I'd been summoned.

Past the busy secretaries, past the line of students waiting for Mr.
Taggert, I made my way to the principal's door.

It was a big corner office, the type that the president of the company
gets. Apart from the massive oak desk the furnishings were sparse. From
the walls gazed generations of principals. Old Mackenzie Bowell himself
presided in oil, sourly contemplating this use of his illustrious name.

"About those letters." Mr. O'Reilly tipped back his chair, lifting his feet almost off the ground. "I know there are some positive things in those letters, but I'm afraid the chief would see only the negative. I'm afraid he'd go after me. He could withdraw some of the services we get." His eyes jumped to the window, perhaps expecting to see a cruiser cautioning him from the driveway. "If some good could come of it I'd say yes, but the trouble with the police is, they're, well, they're vindictive."

I had a sudden picture of the kindly policeman who had come to our house when I was a child, selling tickets to the Policemen's Ball. The polite policeman who gave, then withdrew, my speeding ticket. I could understand my students being suspicious, but why him?

"Don't overestimate the police, Jill. Some of them are graduates of Bowell."

Mr. O'Reilly was explaining to the class why he wouldn't permit the letters to be sent. "If you want to send a letter to the police, send it from your own home. And sign it. Then risk that the person who gets it might not be a mature adult. You might get hassled. That's the danger." He leaned unhappily against the blackboard.

Danger? That wasn't the purpose of the exercise! From my desk in the third row my hand lifted on reflex, before the adult in me lowered it. I took a deep breath. "I . . . would like to differ with Mr. O'Reilly. I think this is a country where we are permitted to criticize." I peeked at him out of the corner of my eye. Somewhere, far away, I could see my father seated at the head of the long dinner table. "Sure, it's not a perfectly free country; I suppose the police could hassle you for your letter; but, if they do, there's recourse to a police review board." His neck was reddening. "And if that doesn't work, there is other legal recourse. And shouldn't we have the courage to speak up?" Between wisps of hair even his scalp burned.

I'd contradicted him. In front of the students. Broken the bonds of authority, as the kids would if they sent their letters. The cops had power, they could hurt the kids.

He had power too.

The terse summons from Mr. O'Reilly in my mail-box confirmed my suspicions: I'd ruined any chance for a job next year. Maybe, on some level, that was what I'd been hoping for – someone to make that difficult choice for me. I wasn't a quitter – I'd stuck it out through the hard fall, the weary winter. And yes, there'd been some small successes. But did I want another year dominated by frustration?

Before I received my termination, however, it was important to speak to him as an equal, to try to make him understand what had been behind my challenge in the classroom.

I stood before the big oak desk. It was a hurdle I had to clear. I forced myself to look squarely into his eyes. "I'm sorry if I embarrassed you in front of the class. It's just that . . . what I was trying to say is . . . by not letting them send their letters we reinforce their paranoia. You know, that the cops are out to get them, that teachers are narcs."

"Paranoia?" His face was round with smiles – he *looked* friendly enough. "They're realistic! Two policemen came into the last school I was at and posed as caretakers. The kids knew they were cops immediately."

"But how could they tell?" My mind was momentarily distracted by this mysterious talent.

He made a motion of pushing a mop briskly. "Because they worked so hard."

We laughed, and I felt more at ease. Perhaps Mr. O'Reilly's friendliness was intended to lessen the impact of the bad news, like a delicious meal before an execution. With nothing to lose, I forged ahead. "Mr. O'Reilly, did you ever receive any, ah . . . complaints . . . about my teaching?"

"Not at all," he said. I looked into his eyes for signs of insincerity. "What I have heard is that you're doing some interesting things with creative writing. I've been meaning to talk to you about it. Did you know that the board has funds available for publishing students' writing? Why don't you consider collecting some of the material and turning it into a book?"

"That would be amazing," I breathed.

"And if there isn't money left for this year, you might consider it for next." His eyes came back to me. "Would you be interested in staying on at Bowell?"

My eyes widened.

"Why don't you think about it. But let me know by graduation."

■

# 29

# TURNING AND TURNING

Ian MacLean, English co-ordinator for the board, was sitting across from me in the staff-room, flipping pages, scanning my students' writing. He looked up. "Names should be put at the bottom, home forms not included. It's all there in the latest issue of *The Magpie's Monthly Treasure*." His tight Scottish burr made the words sting.

He stopped, read one intently, then dropped it on the coffee-table. "Too violent. A lot of people see these books – trustees, board members. . . ."

I looked down. It was a poem about death. Written by David.

And who was Ian MacLean to decide if something was "too violent"? David wrote violently because he *was* violent. He'd punched a violent hole in the door; gone violently out of the school. But his poem was still here.

"What about a cover, and a title?"

"Well . . . I tried to have a contest, but I got only one submission, a sketch of a quill" – I handed it across – "and two titles: 'The Enquiring Quill' and 'The Bowell Book'."

Mr. English Co-ordinator for the Board, I silently addressed his arched brows, have you shoved the special schools into a corner of your mind the way those who attend are shoved into a corner of the system? Have you forgotten that we don't teach Shakespeare, Shaw, T.S. Eliot? That when we have a contest we are lucky to get one submission?

"Mr. MacLean, this is a special school," I said, instead.

"Pardon?"

"It's not a collegiate. It's a special school."

His powdery blue eyes dusted mine. "Well, we can't expect too much then, can we?"

Ian MacLean was back in the staff-room, returning several marked-up pages of my students' writing as examples of how to do layout. "Thirty schools in the borough are publishing creative-writing books this year, but you're the only special school. You've done valiantly, Jill," he added.

I felt I was being patronized; but, to my chagrin, tears of gratitude stung my eyes. My gaze plunged: this year had been hard – so little support in the battle.

But now, at last, I was getting some help. The keyboard class had already typed the poems and stories; kids were arranging, cutting, glueing. Then Mr. MacLean would have them printed and bound.

*The Bowell Book.* How would my students feel when they saw their words published?

The vice-principal's voice crackled over the PA. "There has been" – his voice faltered – "an incident in the parking lot. Will all teachers please identify" – his voice died, was suddenly reborn – "their cars?"

In one motion everyone in the staff-room rose, abandoning the bridge game, the crossword puzzle, the sports section. I glanced back at Ian MacLean stranded in the aisle.

He didn't understand the code.

It looked like the aftermath of a demolition derby: three cars leaning against each other, several askew, their sides smashed, two nose-to-dented-nose, like friendly dogs. Eight, I counted quickly, and mine, thank goodness, not among them.

"Hi, miss." Kevin loosened himself from a knot of kids.

"What happened!"

His eyes shone. "I saw the whole thing! This kid was doin' smoke shows, wanted to squawk his tires a little, and he hit the curb an' lost control." He waved his arm. "Smashed into that car there that smashed into the one beside it that hit the next one. . . ."

Nearby, two teachers stared at their cars in frozen disbelief. I thought of offering condolences, but couldn't find the words. "Who was driving?"

"He took off, he ain't got no licence."

"Kevin." I tore my eyes from the scene. "What are you doing out here?"

"I didn't skip no class, miss, you know I can't do that no more; I was just sittin' with a friend, havin' a beer."

"A beer!"

"Well, maybe two." He smirked.

My eyes were pulled back to the scene. No insurance from the board, wasn't that what Mr. Pritchett had said? And suddenly, wedged between two others, I saw. . . . "My God," I gasped, "isn't that . . . ?"

"Yup!" Kevin concurred happily. "Mr. Pritchett's car. Totalled!"

From behind the wreckage Mr. Pritchett staggered. His mouth moved but emitted no sounds.


Pine needles brushed against the corner of the glass like green feathers. The chuck-chuck sound of nesting birds came faintly in. The sky was bright blue; but Colin's expression, when he turned from the window, was dark.

"I've been thinking about that rocker kid's play you read to me. About what you said."

I sat down by the telephone table. "What do you mean?"

"Do any of us really know what to do with these kids?" His hands flopped open like big, tired wings.

I looked at him in surprise. Humility had never been his trade mark.

"Hit and miss with these kids," he muttered to his hands. "One thing's as good as another. As bad."

I stared. Where was the preacher sermonizing from his book? Was it possible that the guru of clear correct sentences was as conflicted as I?

"So you don't think this system works?"

A snort exploded from his bony nose. "Ah, the question that dares not speak its name!"

I picked up Taggert's pamphlet that had been lying on my desk and mischievously handed it to him. "You mean it's not just a PR problem?"

He glanced at it, shook his head, and chuckled ruefully. "Maybe we should finally face the truth. Stop pretending we're a technical school. What we really are is a rehabilitation centre for the rejects of society. A refuge for the failures of the elementary school system."

"And the kids know it!" I said. "Someone has decided they're dumb enough to be put in here. But unfortunately they're bright enough to understand the implications!"

He looked at me thoughtfully. "Still, think of the alternatives. I remember the days before streaming, when these kids used to be in the regular collegiate classes. They were the slow kids, the angry kids, the ones you kicked out, the ones you failed. They dropped out as soon as they could. And even when they're streamed but stuck in the same school with the other levels, it doesn't work either. They become the Untouchables. That's supposedly why the special schools were created in the first place. To give these kids a chance to succeed on their own terms." He paused. "Whatever that means," he added sardonically. "Give them courses tailored to their own needs—"

"But that's one of the problems!" I interjected. "In the collegiates there are clear guidelines that come down from the ministry. But what are the guidelines for these kids? What are we supposed to be teaching them?"

"As far as I can see, the main message seems to be: 'Make them employable.' So that's what I've tried to do. However," – he studied the moving pattern of the pine – "at the end of four years of drill and exercises, I'm not sure any of it's even stuck. Have I prepared them any better for employment at McDonald's, or pumping gas?" Colin's motor was running down. The shadows were closing in again around him.

I waited. When he resumed, his voice was lower and a sour look puckered his face. "Did you know that I have half my doctorate completed? You're surprised, aren't you?" He seemed to take some perverse pleasure in relaying this news. "Alexander Pope. Gave him up to come to a special school, watch the seed of Chaos grow at first hand." His acidic chuckles died away.

The only sound was of pine needles scraping glass. "Then rose the seed of Chaos and of Night,/To blot out order, and extinguish light,/Of dull and venal a new world to mould. . . ."

"What's that from?"

"*The Dunciad.* Pope's 'Epic of Dunces'." He smirked.

Bleakly I stared at him: a burnt-out case. Was that what would happen to me if I told the principal I'd decided to stay on next year?

But even if the system was deeply flawed, did it have to diminish everyone? Couldn't a good teacher under any system give kids the dignity they needed to learn, to work? Ultimately, didn't it come down to those certain moments: sufficient trust in the classroom, sufficient openness; then the teacher, poised with a concept, seizing that moment; and suddenly blank eyes focusing, faces illuminating, as a spark jumped across the charged air.

"The only answer to this whole streaming issue," Colin said, a wicked grin flickering across his face, "is early retirement."

The telephone message was in my mail-box. I steeled myself.

"Miss Solnicki," Dori's voice sang. "Guess what! I'm gettin' married!"

"Oh, Dori." My spirits sank.

"Beginning of June."

"So soon!"

"Yeah! Isn't it great?"

"It's really . . . something. Are you going on a . . . ?" I was supposed to speak of "ring," "shower," "trip"; but the words were jagged, they wouldn't slip out of my mouth.

"Honeymoon?"

"Yes."

"Well, what with Neil bein' laid off, and we want to spend our money on, yah know, a sofa and stuff, we're gonna wait, go on a cruise or somethin' later."

So she really was getting married.

"What's your address?" She giggled nervously. "I'd like to send yah an invitation to our Jack-'n'-Jill party. Could yah come?"

"Gee Dori, thanks, but I don't know." This little girl with a fractured wrist and stitches, who said I was her best friend. . . . "Well, I'll try."

"Great!" she bubbled. "So I'll be seein' yah soon!"

Another word I couldn't say: Congratulations.


I screeched into the parking lot, grabbed my overloaded briefcase, and made a dash for the school. I was late, but with good reason: I'd stopped by the board office to pick up the proofs, hot off the press, for *The Bowell Book*. Now the kids could make another contribution: proofreading and correcting.

I raced down the corridor, empty save for Dino and a few other late-comers still fidgeting at their lockers. As I passed, Dino spun towards me. "Miss, did yah hear what happened?"

"Not now, Dino, I'm late," I called over my shoulder.

I turned into the classroom. The kids were all pressing around one desk. "Holy shit!" I heard Christie's voice say. "I can't believe it's him!"

"Who?" I pushed my way through to the desk. All eyes were riveted on a copy of the *Sun*, on a headline that leaped out: "FIVE TEENS KILLED IN POLICE CHASE CRASH." Beneath it a huge photo of the wreckage. And his name, pummelling me from all sides.

"Him" was David.

Kevin recited the details: boys driving down the 401 in a stolen car. Alcohol or drugs. The police gave chase. The boys saw cruisers blocking the highway ahead. They did a U-turn, headed back, going west in the eastbound lanes. Hit a truck head-on.

David. David was dead.

"And get *this*! His mom was there, in the very same hospital they took him to, at the very same time."

I was staring at Kevin, but I was seeing a frail back retreating down the hall, a door closing on it. A swirling babble overpowered the real voices around me: "turned around this year thanks to you"; "control myself"; "bye . . . Mom"; "David deleted. David deleted. David deleted."


At last, the final bell. I shoved *The Bowell Book* proofs back into my briefcase and headed home. What was the point of teaching these kids? A dead-end job, preparing them for their dead-end jobs, their dead-end lives, so they could wind up just plain dead.

Thirty-six days – I'd counted – until it was all over.

■

From the composition program:

**FIRST POEM**

**LIFE**

I look out the window at the red leafs on the trees, at the pure driven snow, at the green opening buds, and wounder, how does it work? it is like a chain, . . . the world is like a chain it just keeps turning and turning even with the hurt, the violence, the love.

Peter

# 30

# CHANGES

I really didn't want to go. So why was I going? I guess it was because I felt I owed it to Dori, to our friendship. I pulled up to the small brick bungalow and, clutching my gift, walked past the three motorcycles parked in the driveway. How long before those boys would smash themselves to bits?

"Miss Solnicki! You came!" Dori screamed at the door. She led me past a narrow kitchen where several women were preparing food, to an L-shaped living- and dining-area. A folded sign on the table said: BEER $2.50; SCOTCH $3.50. I'd never been to a house where people charged for drinks.

"Have some punch." Dori's mother came up with a smile. She was a plump, pretty woman, in her mid-thirties, her Irish accent still strong. "It's free," she added. Had she caught me staring at the sign?

"Punch, I'll give yah a punch," a man said, at my elbow. Curly hair and a snub nose gave him a boyish look, despite his florid cheeks.

"Get on with ye," Dori's mother said to her husband. "This here is Mrs. Solonacki, Dori's teacher." He grinned and handed me a glass.

I found a chair and slipped into it, sipping my punch self-consciously. In the corner an older boy was calling, like a barker: "Forget the food – it's free; have a drink, we'll even deliver it to yah!" I recognized him from a wedding picture on the buffet, the one beside the portrait of Prince Charles, Princess Di, and their children.

In the corner, Dori was flirting with one of the long-haired young men. She rose on tiptoes in her stiletto heels and lightly kissed him. The men all stared at her tight miniskirt riding up. "Hey, Neil, better keep an eye on her," Dori's father called out.

The fat man in the next chair turned. "Solnick. . . ." He tasted it as if it were a foreign food. "What kinda name is that?"

"Ah . . . my husband's parents came from Poland."

His tongue crawled across his lips. "That wouldn't happen to be a Jewish name now, would it?"

I felt the denial rising within me. But why should I hide from this jerk? Why should I give in to this game of ignorance and stupidity, conceal a part of myself in my own Secret Annexe? Suddenly I heard myself say: "As a matter of fact, it is."

"Now she's Jewish, so watch yourself!" Dori's mother cautioned loudly at my side, as everyone turned to look. "None o' your Jewish jokes!"

I sat stiffly in my chair while my neighbour obliged and talked about his health. "Doctor told me fifteen years ago if I didn't give up drinkin' I'd be dead in six months. Jewish doctor," he added, to make known what a supporter of Jews he was. He held up his wrist, clamped with a green plastic bracelet, as if he'd been discharged from the hospital directly to this party. "First thing every mornin' I have a shot o' rye. Mind you," he added, seeing my look of surprise, "I don't *eat* nuthin'." He took a drink from Dori's father, and reached towards his pocket. "It's on me," Dori's father said.

"Pardon me if I drink it in the glass, instead of on you." He gave me a broad wink.

Dori and Neil were opening presents, and I turned to watch. "Read the card!" someone called out.

"He can't read," Dori said. Neil's face coloured.

"That's why yah invited a teacher, so she could read the cards!" someone shouted. Everyone laughed while I shifted uncomfortably. I was the Jewish Teacher: I didn't belong here.

Dori unwrapped a set of six glass plates. "They'll make great frisbees," her older brother, the drink-seller, said. She tossed back her blond bangs, and for a moment I saw the puckers of her stitches, like shadows. She raised a plate and took aim at Neil. "I'll throw 'em at him, one at a time," she said.

"Come on, come on," he grinned. "Just try it, and wham!" He punched the air between them.

"Atta boy, Neil, show her who's boss!" the fat man called from his ringside seat, as everyone laughed.

"Thanks for coming," Dori said at the door.

"Good luck," I said, stifling my sadness. I took her hands in mine and looked into her face. She was what she was. Leaning forward, I kissed her on the cheek. Teacher's lips, student's cheek: now we were both women. "Have lots, and lots, of luck."

I stared out the car window into the darkening spring night. I had always thought of Dori as the victim. But now I had seen the look in her eyes as she'd raised that plate.

"Know how to keep cool?" Peter said, pulling himself past some broken glass from the window above and leaning back against the wall, out of the sun. Around the corner came giggles and the music of a portable radio.

He put down his book, held up a long pink Freezee, and touched it to his wrist. "Yah put the ice here. Feel it." He placed my fingers on his pulse. "The baby heart takes the cold blood to your big heart, cools the whole body."

I was glad to touch his wrist. He'd been upset because he had no money for today's school outing to Canada's Wonderland.

"Hey, miss," he said suddenly, "where'd yah go to high school?"

I dropped his wrist. "Ah . . . Forest Hill Collegiate."

His face scrunched up. "Where's that?"

He didn't know. He wouldn't suddenly see me in a new way, his vision forever altered by a word. "Downtown."

"Why'd you go to a *collegiate?*" He peered through the haze in his grey eyes.

I shrugged. "I guess I wanted to go to university."

He studied me as if I were a peculiar object he'd just found beside him in the grass. "Why?"

How could I explain that, where I came from, university naturally followed high school the way night followed day. "I just . . . went! Anyway, I couldn't have become a teacher if I hadn't."

"So is that why?"

"Not really." He could never understand that, for me and many other women in those days, teaching had lain at the end of a degree like a comfortable bed – little preparation to get into, little fuss to get out of, or to make part-time use of once you had children. It dovetailed with the main agenda: marriage and family.

His eyes narrowed. "Were you one of them browners?"

I smiled enigmatically. I certainly wouldn't tell him about my scholarships.

"I got a friend goes to Pearson Collegiate, he's a goof, a Newfie!" He spat out his contempt. "So why would you want to go to a *collegiate?*" he repeated.

The real explanation was one I didn't want to spell out, the business of being programmed into a particular future: into a collegiate, or a basic-level school. Canada wasn't India, with its caste system, or Britain, with its class system. Social barriers weren't supposed to exist here. But they did. "Once on welfare, always on welfare." Wasn't that why Peter despaired? I was understanding more and more that it would take an exceptional person to overcome this system.

"It's too hot," he said suddenly, getting up. He went through the open door and back into the class-room.

After a while I got up, too. I looked into the open area. Into an empty room.

He was gone. He'd skipped off. Not that I blamed him, with everyone else away, the May sky and leafy trees holding out their invitation. But it made me angry anyway; his setting me up, betraying me like that.

Then, up near the front, I heard a murmur. I tiptoed nearer. In a carrel, Peter was bent intently over his book – eyes squinting, mouth working, finger trekking across the page.

Silently I stood and watched as, step by step, he struggled up a mountain towards a distant peak where hard books were easy, and welfare no more.


From a journal:

> **im goin to be Unset for awhile cause of a Good Friend**
> **dying. i still cant beleave that david is Dead. i keep telling**

myself that its not david it was Someone else i keep tryin
to think that but i gess it was Him, hes not breething
moving or even talking. i had a Dream last nite about
david, i woke with tears down my eyes.

Cammy

For the last nine days (I was still counting) David's death had moved
from a shocking, distressing event to one that provoked discussion.
Everyone had an opinion. Mr. Taggert: "I keep thinking, was there something we could have done?" Mr. Pritchett: "I don't blame the system, I
blame the parents. We didn't fail *them*, they failed *us*."

Christie hung back after the junior English class. "D'you remember
what I wrote in my journal, a while ago, about needin' to change?" She
tossed back her brown hair, a confident gesture that reminded me of
how she used to be. "Well, David couldn't change. He was . . . sorta
stuck."

Each time, his name stabbed. It was hard to shake the feeling that I'd
failed him. If I'd been a better teacher, a haunting voice said, known how
to render the right life-saving breath. . . .

But another voice agreed with Christie. The plan had been sketched
long before I got there. That voice comforted me. Maybe doctors heard
it when their patients died. Or social workers, or. . . .

I changed the subject. "How are things going with you, Christie?"

Her face broadened with joy. "I've been meanin' to tell yah! They
found us an apartment, we move out next week! And we're gonna get a
Samoyed, we're pickin' it up from my uncle this weekend."

Christie was leaving the shelter! I wanted to fold her in my arms and
share her happiness. *Somebody* had escaped.

In my mind I saw a white dog running, running through the high
green grass.

Peter held up the slim volume. "I finished the book, miss! I finished the
book!" He ran around the room waving it in the air, oblivious to Dino's
and Randy's smirks. His skin glowed pink, its characteristic pallor banished. "First time I ever finished a book in my life!"

Day after day I had watched him, a cripple, one foot in front of the other as he painfully hobbled where others ran.

"So what do I haveta do now? Write a book report? Yah finish a book and yah write a book report, right? Everyone does that," he added, as if all over the world people on their sofas, in bed, stretched out on the beach, put down the just-completed book and reached for the foolscap.

But I couldn't ask him to write one of those analytical, dull, collegiate-type reports. "Did you like it?" I asked.

He looked doubtful. "It was okay." He turned it over and studied the endorsements on the back. "Not as good as they said it was."

"Why not write to the author or the publisher? Give them your opinion. Then imagine what they would write back."

**BOOK REPORT**

Title – All About Werewolves
To Who this has Concerned.
I am writing this letter to you to speak my Opinion about
your Novel.
I feel this book is highly eggsagerated. This book never
gives you one word of proof that werewolves do or did
exist. Also when you pick up the book and you read the
print on the back cover, the book apears to be quiet
interesting. But then you get reading the book and it
changes its story and that makes you confused and that
a noise me, after all I picked up your Novel thinking that
I could enjoy reading it for pleasure and maybe a little
info, about the werewolf.
I hope you will anser.

Your's Truely,
Peter Cagney

■■■

Dear Mr Cagney,
Im sorry to hear that you did not care to much for our
Novel. Our book was not written to please everybody after
all its a big world. Actually the mujority of letters I have

recieved have been fairly reviewed as one of the best Novels on the shelves. As for the outline on the back cover you said the book apeared to be interesting, but as you read the Novel you say that it confused you. Quiet frankly Mr Cagney I feel that the book was strait forward. I would suggest that you read a book that is within your vocabaluary.

> Sinseerly,
> the Publisher

I stared at the title: It wasn't *Never Cry Wolf*, but Peter *had* stuck to his resolve to read a book about wolves, of sorts.

Hadn't I once thought my students were wolves, circling? I hadn't been able to see, then, that the flip side of the Wolf was the Peter, a boy trying to be brave under duress. And how had I been able to get past the bared fangs, flattened ears, to the vulnerable boy?

Through writing.

Before me, Randy's face formed into a crisp, purple, vanished ten-dollar bill; then it re-formed as pasty skin and pimples. Dramatically he touched a scratch on his cheek. "Almost had all the niggers in the school on me at lunch today."

"Blacks," I corrected.

"You can call 'em that if you want."

"Yes, that's what I want!"

"Whatever they are, they almost *killed* me!" Now everyone had gathered around this warrior returned from lunch.

"What happened?" Dino asked, admiring the scratch.

"This nig – this *black* guy," he grinned at me, "bumped into me in the caf, made my chips fly all over. So I said, 'Ya God damn fuckin' nigger asshole, it's yer fault!' It was okay, it was cool," he added, confirming the casual inoffensiveness of the remark. "Then this big, fuckin' dude takes off his shirt, he's got muscles where I didn't even think yah could have 'em! And all of a sudden a whole table of 'em stands up and they pull out knives, and I'm thinkin' this is gonna be my last minute on earth, and" –

he paused dramatically to extend the moment's spell – "d'yah know what saved me?"

"What?" It was a collective sigh.

"Leroy! Guy I useta be on the track team with before that bastard Sawchuk kicked me off. He comes over, says to the big dude, 'It was yer fault. Yah touch him and you'll haveta fight me.'"

His voice filled with wonder, "I never thought there'd come a day I'd be defended by a fuckin' . . . *black!*"


"Hey, miss, d'yah know why Jews got big ears and bald heads? Cuz they go 'What's the price?'" – Ray tugged his ears – "and 'Oh my God!'" – he ran his fingers through his hair.

Not this again! I put down the book we were reading. "Say it!" a voice whispered. I drew myself up straight, struggling to quell the thunder in my chest, stop my throat from constricting, as if it were refusing to speak. "How many of you actually have met someone . . . Jewish?"

Two hands went up.

"Well . . . now you all have. I'm Jewish." I leaned heavily against the blackboard.

"What'd she say?" a voice cried.

"She said she's Jewish!" The word raced through the class, fire fanned by wind.

"Hey, you wear one of them beanie things?"

"You talk in that crazy language?"

"Don't yah believe in God?"

"You have them stars with little candle things in 'em?"

"Menorahs," I said.

"Menorarahs," he repeated.

"You from Jerusalem?"

"My grandmother immigrated from the Ukraine."

"So you're Jewish, but you're not a Jew."

"My religion is Jewish, my nationality is Canadian."

"That's why she dresses Mexican – Jews an' Mexicans, they're the same thing."

Ray leaned back in his seat. "You're a Jew? Shit, you're a Jew? And I was just gettin' to like you. Shit, I thought I could tell a Jew."

"I could tell," someone said. "When you told us, I looked at you, I knew." He nodded wisely. "It's the eyes."

A girl laughed. "You know how you always ask for collateral when you give out pencils? You don't give nuthin' away for nuthin', right? Jews are cheap."

"No, she's not, she's generous." The Good News Bible Girl interced-ed on my behalf. It was fifteenth-century Spain: I stood before the Supreme Council of the Inquisition. "You've got a very giving personality, miss."

"Yeah, and yah don't advertise, yer not like them Jews that go from door to door sellin' things and handin' out papers."

"Every creature of God is good, and nothing to be refused," added the Good News Bible Girl.

Ray studied me from his seat. "Shit, you're a pretty nice Jew, miss. I met some who aren't, but you're okay." I frowned at him. "Don't get me wrong, miss, I got nuthin' against Jews; it's just that the ones I met I never like. I never met a nice Jew."

"Well, now you have."

"One."

I looked away. I hadn't made a dent. Still, revealing myself hadn't been as painful as I feared.

I took an immense breath, for strength. "You know how I'm always asking you to write in your journals? Tomorrow I'd like to read to you from a famous journal. It was written by a Jewish girl, in Holland, during the Second World War. Because Jews were being persecuted by the Nazis, and many millions were being killed, she and her family went into hiding. She kept a diary during that time.

"Her name was Anne Frank."


I jerked up in bed, my heart a beating drum. In the dream I had been walking down the school corridor wearing a towel. But the towel was small, it covered only my front. All the kids were pointing and laughing at my naked backside. Even David was laughing.


Anne, you rise from the dark grave of my briefcase, your young face reaching out from the book cover for air, sky, the chestnut tree, the clock at Westertoren, this spring day that you deeply inhale as I begin reading. . . .

> Saturday, 20 June, 1942: . . . It's an odd idea for someone like me to keep a diary . . . because it seems to me that neither I – nor for that matter anyone else – will be interested in the unbosomings of a thirteen-year-old schoolgirl. Still, what does that matter? I want to write, but more than that, I want to bring out all kinds of things that lie buried deep in my heart.

Only the wall clock ticking, pages rustling, Anne's clear unwavering voice speaking from weeks and months of confinement in that attic, out into the silence.

> Saturday, 15 July, 1944: . . . It's really a wonder that I haven't dropped all my ideals, because they seem so absurd and impossible to carry out. Yet I keep them, because in spite of everything I still believe that people are really good at heart. . . . I see the world gradually being turned into a wilderness, I hear the ever-approaching thunder, which will destroy us too, I can feel the sufferings of millions and yet. . . .

I stopped. "That was the third-last entry in her diary." I steadied my voice, willed it to stop quavering. "Not long after that the police burst in on them."

"How was it found, miss?"

"Of the family, and the others, only Anne's father survived the concentration camps." I waited, then went on. "He returned to Amsterdam after the war. Miep and Elli gave him Anne's notebooks and papers that they found on the floor of the Secret Annexe after . . . after everyone was taken away. He . . . circulated the diary privately, for a few friends, as a memorial." My voice faltered. "And people read it, and. . . ." I began to cry. I was sobbing, sobbing, I couldn't stop. "I'm sorry. It means so much to me."

The merciful bell. They rose from their seats, passed me, quietly casting glances or looking discreetly away, like those who understand, like friends.

Then, outside, I heard the triumphant voice trumpet: "OUR TEACHER CRIED!"

But another voice answered: "AH, SHUT UP!"

■

From a journal:

> Two or three years ago my brother told me something that would change some of my feelings towrad him, that would shock me, embarrass me but most of all bother me.
>
> My brother told me he was gay.
>
> We were sitting in a movie theater we were ten minutes early I told him that some of my friends were saying that if a guy wear a earing on the right side it means he's gay. He told me it was true for some people then I realised that he had a earing on the right side. I waited for the movie to start then I said loud almost screaming (I was scared) I said Hey are you a cissy? He said Hey! then I said is that why you don't have a girlfriend he said Yey!
>
> I wanted to talk to somebody anybody but for some reason not him then the movie ended. As we were walking out I said to myself well if he's happy I should be to. I said Hey there must be someone elses brother whose gay he said Hey lots! with a smile.
>
> Then I ask him does anybody know he said mom and dad and my sister to but granddad and grandma didn't know and still dont then I said What does dad think He doesn't like it he said.
>
> Then I said Okay my boy lets go get a pizza thats if you're still a boy. Before I could finish he said I changed but not that much!
>
> I love my brother very much I told him it was okay

about being gay and all because if one member of my family isn't happy I'm not either.

So if people think a gay guy is stupid and weak phsicly and mentaly they are wrong because you havn't met my brother he's the best brother friend a person can have.

Nadine

P.S. My second cousins husbands aunt is jewish to.

31

## THE BOWELL BOOK

I pushed through morning teacher gossip and made my way to my mailbox. As I sorted through memos, Nick Sawchuk was announcing: "Twenty-one days to go!" It seemed others were counting down, too. Around me swirled summer talk: cottages, boats, camping trips, travel. Only a set of exams stood in the way.

"From the board office," one of the secretaries called, pointing to three cartons sitting against the wall. Under the packing that I tore away were stacks of shiny bindings, an arching quill, a scripted title.

Excitedly I penned the announcement I would broadcast over the PA: "*The Bowell Book* has arrived!"

At 3:01 the first contributors timidly peered through the door of the English office. I beckoned. Gingerly, they stepped across the border.

I gestured to a table, now covered in blue-and-gold books. Suspiciously they looked, tentatively they touched; it was, after all, a book. Then came an explosion, the coil spine creaking, the pages whooshing, until they came, at last, to *their* page, *their* name. . . .

"Hey, look, I'm famous!"

"Gonna make millions!"

"Want my autograph?" Clive shoved a book under my nose.

I stayed past the last ebullient shout, slam of door, jingle of keys, swish of a janitor's broom. It was 5:00 p.m., the hour when the ghosts come.

David first. Slowly I turned to his poem. We'd included it, outlined in black, as a memorial. In one explosive shudder of the clock's hand he'd been obliterated. But on this page he was still alive.

Now Dori's love poem, with its youthful innocence. Soon she'd be marrying Neil. But at least, under these covers, the girl was safe from harm.

Here was scary Jack – who'd disappeared down the hall, to where? – and Peter's group home, Angie's dead father, all the cinquains and lists and plays and stories.

I laid my head on the cool oak of the desk. Who knew where my students would end up? Or, for that matter, where I was going?

But at this moment it didn't seem to matter. Because together we had made something to hold, something lasting.


The police car was a flicker in the corner of my eye, the two cops a dark blur, as I raced towards the auditorium, late for the Athletic Awards Assembly. Just as I reached the door, one of them stopped me.

"Excuse me, ma'am, you a teacher here?" I nodded. "D'you know this kid?" I looked down at the picture and saw a familiar grin; I raised my eyes to the stage, where, at that very moment, the same grin was beaming out at the audience as Mr. O'Reilly proclaimed: "For outstanding achievement in sports, the trophy for Athlete of the Year: Leroy Whitney!"

Their eyes widening with the shock of recognition, the cops pushed past the door. I touched one of them on the arm. "At least let him get his award. Come on. . . ."

He shook his head. "Now it makes sense! This kid's up for shoplifting. He's the ringleader of a gang that swarmed a store at the Eaton Centre. No wonder he's so hard to catch – all he has to do is grab the clothes and run!"

Bearing his trophy, Leroy marched triumphantly down the stairs. Suddenly he spotted the uniforms moving towards him. He froze. Then, spinning, he sprinted for the exit, clutching the trophy like a football.

"God damn!" The policeman hurled his pencil to the floor. "We lost him again!"

Mr. Taggert swivelled around in his chair. The weight of an almost-finished year had crushed his shoulders. "Athlete of the Year." He shook his head and gave the pile of Referral Room forms a particularly nasty jab.

The sweet smell of marijuana drifted into the room. Somebody was leaning against the bricks, gazing dreamily at the sky; we could catch him if we went out. Mr. Taggert got up and closed the window.

"Here," I said. I laid *The Bowell Book* gently down on his desk.

Slowly he opened it and began to turn the pages. Soon he was flipping faster, faster.

The current had switched on in his eyes. Now he raised the blue-and-gold book aloft and waved it like a flag, as if to lead his exhausted troops back into battle. His hair was a crimson beacon. "We'll send it to the elementary schools, to the collegiates, to the trustees! By God, it'll be great Public Relations!"

"Have you seen *The Bowell Book?*" Colin asked.

Mr. Pritchett was in an even worse mood than usual. The insurance company had paid for his car but greatly increased his premiums. I braced myself for his response: only seventeen days to go.

He lifted his darkening face from the chicken pot pie. "I had the pleasure. Some of the stories and poems in there. . . ." He snipped a corner of the crust. "I'm surprised the board accepted them."

These kids: outcasts from the world of words. And now, by putting together their own book, they'd been let in. Now they could appreciate the reasons behind the writing of others, now no longer view books with suspicion.

"Actually, they were pretty cleaned up. You should have seen them before." I grinned.

"Several *did* fall into my hands during the year. Awarded As, I might add, instead of G for garbage." He dabbed his mouth with a napkin.

I threw my napkin to the table like a gauntlet. "You know, Mr. Pritchett, these kids have been torn down all their lives – teachers pummelling them with their mistakes, their families falling apart. They told

236 | THE REAL ME IS GONNA BE A SHOCK

me they feel like *rejects!* They need affirmation! It's to get them to *like* writing that I've not dwelled on grammar, to get them to like *themselves.*"

Colin had been listening in silence. Suddenly he pushed back his chair. "I agree," he said.

I turned towards him. With whom did he agree?

"It's true Jill's students don't always write clear, correct sentences." He wagged his finger like a reproving department head. "From that point of view, it may be garbage. But . . . it's beautiful garbage!"

He was smiling at me.


A visiting band from a nearby collegiate sat tidily in the pit. The young musicians' uniforms were ironed, their hair clipped. The conductor raised his baton, and they began with a medley from *Carmen.* A collective groan rose from the audience. Now Elgar's "Pomp and Circumstance." The audience looked like it might mutiny.

Suddenly the curtains opened, and there on stage was a steel-drum band – black kids, white kids, and a teacher. The audience let out a whoop.

Calypso. It carried the scent of hibiscus, papaya, salt-spray on the skin, and a red sun drowning in the sea that rocked, rolled, beat against the beach.

Three rows of black heads were swaying in front of me, arms raised, fingers jabbing the air, when the entire row suddenly was yanked up by strings of sound. Hands linking waists, they began to wind up the side of the room. Another row lifted, another; more kids jumped to their feet to join the ever-lengthening line. Down the middle aisle and up the sides it weaved, not just black heads and brown limbs, but pink legs kicking, pale hands reaching; and now – could that be Nick Sawchuk squeezed between two ample black girls? and Mr. Pritchett dragged reluctantly to his feet? and, yes, a beaming Mr. Taggert, too? All at once the snake surged up the stairs to the stage. A pony-tailed player abandoned her drum. Now the stage was a roiling mass as people clung to one another, differences forgotten in the glad calypso beat.

32

## GRADUATION

From journals:

> Well, soon Im graduating. Im gonna miss Bowell. Never
> thot Id say that!? My futur plans are as follows
> 1, live through my 19 birthday
> 2, buy myself a Harley Davidson and an old lady
> 3, find a good paying job.

■ ■ ■

> Last July my grandfather & grandmother were up at their
> trailer until grandfather had to rush grandmother to the
> Hospital. On the way she died. That was my first funeral.
> The second funeral was in March where my grandfather on
> my dads side died in the hospital with five machines on
> him tring to keep him alive but at 10:53 pm the line on the
> heart machine just went straight. So thats why some times
> I look like I am in a daise. I am just thinking how could
> they not see me on graduation with a suit. But I know that
> they are going to be their somewhere. I will just have to
> prove to them that I did it all by myself.

■ ■ ■

> I closed my eyes and wished. When I opened them it was
> graduation night. It was special moment for us all.

My father and mother was proud of me when I was on the stand saying my speech. My speech was 15 minutes long. Every word was well spoken for. After I finished I received what I was waiting for a long time, my graduating diploma, when I felt it and looked at it my eyes was full of tears.

After the graduation my parents and I went out to celebrate. We went to a restront and had a special graduation feist. My parents and I were talking about my future plans. I told them I will go to College for two years and study Electronics. My parents are pleased because it is a good carere and it makes good money. When my parents and I left the restrant we went home. I went to bed because it was a long night, but I couldn't sleep because the night was so cherishable.

Countdown. Six days left before exams. Hot, humid, I was swimming down the halls. From a distance, Hilda looked like a whale.

"Randy Edwards came to see me today," Mr. Taggert said. "Told me he just got a job and wanted to quit school."

"He quit?" I said, incredulous. "He was finally going to graduate!" Mr. Taggert's helpless giggles bubbled as he nodded.

Five days.

Three students stood separate, silent, staring through the glass of the front foyer.

"What's there?" I also turned to look.

"Outside."

Four days.

Every night the janitor secured the windows, a screw in each corner. Every morning the kids entered the sweltering room, brought out their knives, removed those screws.

Water bombs falling from the second storey splashed in. People leaned in, their elbows on the sill. A pine cone sailed by me as if the pine tree had launched it. A pop can barely missed someone's head.


Two days.

Smell of smoke. A pile of ashes by the wall, near the foyer door. I bent down, made out scorched paper, a curl of cardboard, one intact hole. The ritual burning of a notebook. I stepped back. Now it was a pile of crows' feathers.


I watched bobbing heads and hands as the kids hunched over their desks. It was the creative-writing exam, our last time together. I wanted to make a speech, say thank you, goodbye. And have those things said to me: "On behalf of everyone here I'd like to thank Mrs. Solnicki. . . ."

But they had already handed in their foolscap, walked out, tossing an occasional goodbye over their shoulders like a jacket discarded on a warm day. Now the room stared back, empty but for the folded packets in front of me on the desk.

I opened one and read it. From the hallway came laughter, a low "Fuck!" Feet tapped towards the staff-room. I read another. Another. Another. . . .

A breeze blew in from the window, making the spots of sunlight dance. Something rare had happened. Was it because they were graduating, caught at an end, suspended before a beginning, that today they spoke so openly of the things that lie buried in the heart?

#### WINDOWS

Windows are beutiful
there like the sun of a room
I watch as a small fly bounces
off the clear glass again and again
If only he knew the purpose of a window –
To let things in and keep them out.

■ ■ ■

WORKING

Working is like working for nothing, taking orders
from difrent people getting paid underrate
Moving here and there to make a living. Working
is really just to keep your life span going
you hardly make any money for yourself,
You've got to pay for almost every thing you need.
It's like a little game, Working
to enjoy life pleasure.

■ ■ ■

DREAMS

I hate having dreams
You have good ones you have bad ones
In my case I never have good dreams
I have dreams bein a little kid again
lost out in the city
I have dreams of standing in the
middle of the road and a car
coming at me and I can not move
I have dreams that actualy happen
I had a dream I got in a car
accident sure enough it happened the next day
I had a dream that my aunt
died and they couldn't find out
how she died sure enough it happened
the same way as my dream
Some of my dreams really upset me
like I dream all the time of being at my
mom's funeral, my dad's funeral.
All I hoping for is at least
one good dream.

■ ■ ■

THE FOREST

I envy the forest which I have seen
the green leaves whistling way up in the trees
the smell of fresh pine giving brightness
to the big blue sky.
The animals do as they wish
with no dispare.
I wish I could live with the air in the trees!

···

CHANGE OF TIME

Walking through a forest drunk as hell,
sweet aroma of Columbian is all you smell,

The ripe age of fourteen I took time in stride,
a bottle in one hand, a girl at my side.

Now things are different and time it seems,
has delt me a bad hand in life and dreams.

I have to fight
to get things right.

···

SPACE

Drifting around like a helpless boat in the middle
     of the ocean
and the only sound you hear is your heart
beating like waves against the boat
just drifting and your bound to go insain
because you have nobody to talk to
as if you were dum and deaf and always wondering
where in the hell youll end up.

■■■

PICTURES IN MY MIND

There is this little picture
In the back of my mind
It is like a human face
That realy isn't there.

This picture really scares me
It is like a body with no head
Beacuse everytime I look at it
The face realy isn't there.

■■■

SPIN

Left alone waiting for someone
to help me out of my past
and into the future,
a sholder to cry on,
a friend who cares.
The world goes around and lives change
but for me it stands still.

If only I had a long enough string
I would wrap up the world,
spin it like a top,
then maybe the world
would spin for me.

■■■

SCHOOL

School is like youth,
You grow up quickly and learn the truth.
They say these are the best years of our lives,

Now I see they were not lies.
I've learned from many, and I've learned
    from few,
Soon I'll be out with nothing to do.

So help me someone
For I am lost,

I need more time
To stop those clocks.

I know it won't happen
So now I regret
All those mistakes
I will never forget.

I am not sad

            Just scared.

        ■■■

SCHOOLS END

Clean out your lockers
take everything home
have a year end party
get the phone numbers you always wanted
say good ridance to teachers
cry over boyfriends
Next year will be different
New boyfriends New friends
it may be scary
it may be great
but wether they like it or not
everyone will be changed.

Ray and a buddy were leaning against the rad in the front foyer when I came out. "Sorry I didn't hand in a poem, Miss Solnicki." Mutely I nodded, acknowledging the disappointment I'd felt when I faced his blank page. "But I *am* gonna do it. I'll give it to yah at graduation."

The boys looked uncomfortable in their suits and tuxedos, the girls sweetly awkward in gowns and high heels. One by one they got up from their seats in the front rows and climbed the stairs to receive the rolled diploma from Mr. O'Reilly's outstretched hand. Behind him sat the serious, straight-backed department heads, trustees, superintendents, and other assorted dignitaries. Before him was the sweating, whispering, shuffling, standing-up, and sitting-down throng of parents, grandparents, friends, and small squirming brothers and sisters.

Now the local school trustee came forward to address the crowd. "When I stand here and look out over this group of fine graduates, it confirms to me again the value of the special schools, where the less-than-gifted can succeed. . . ." No one in the cafetorium listened, not one face behind a fanning program reacted, except for the principal, who looked embarrassed, coughed into his hand.

Another in the line of speakers, a pastor dressed in sombre cloth. "You are at a crossroads," he intoned to the graduates, "leaving one way of life, moving to another. . . ."

All those days I'd been counting down had not prepared me for this feeling of sadness, or for the images that came tumbling through my mind.

David pushing the glass door.

"Your dreams may be as diverse as two stones lying on the ground . . ."

Dori turning back towards her future husband.

". . . but you must make it happen, you must throw the stone across the water. . . ."

Peter's finger journeying across the page.

As if to reinforce the pastor's words, the school orchestra embarked on Dvorak's *New World Symphony*. It's true that the strings floundered through the Great Lakes, the horns stumbled over the Alleghenies, the clarinets squeaked across the desert towards Santa Fe; but what did it matter as long as they really had crossed the water, stepped on to the shore of a new, waiting world? A mother beside me turned her worn face to mine, and smiled.

The crowd spilled out of the hot stuffiness into the hall. Couples held hands. Several girls were pregnant, or pushed strollers, as if the future had already swallowed them up. The Good News Bible Girl marched past, humming "Onward Christian Soldiers."

"Peter!" I said, marvelling that no odour accompanied him, that graduation, like baptism, had led him towards water. "You're out in the big wide world now! Are you scared?"

"Miss, I been in the world all the time," he patiently explained. "I just had to come here part-time."

Clive held up a glass of punch. "I was accepted at Laurier, miss! I'm going to a collegiate!" His coal eyes glowed. I went to touch my glass to his. But something else was in his eyes. "I'm really happy." He looked away. "But, I'm gonna miss this place."

The parking lot was almost deserted by the time I came out. I got into the car, but I didn't want to go anywhere. I stared into the falling night. A dark-skinned girl in a white formal, like a camellia in the dusk, got into a van and slammed the door.

On the night of my graduation from Forest Hill Collegiate, I was the winner of three university scholarships. But for all that, was I better, or different, from these kids? All of us were together, struggling for a life, for that feeling at the end, as the shade came finally, gently down, that some hours, some days – if you were lucky, some years – had been well lived. . . .

"She'll really go somewhere," they must have thought, the parents, teachers, fellow students, as I, too, climbed the stairs to the stage. But when I stepped down, I hadn't quite known where to go. University, marriage, children, uncommitted work – the comfortable, safe route. Yet somehow, in some way, I knew now that all those steps had led me here.

Tires squealed, and a battered, blue pick-up truck lurched to a stop alongside my car. Ray leaned out of the driver's window, two girls beside him. His sleeve had changed from black to white, a tuxedo. "Hey, Miss Solnicki," he grinned, "I got somethin' for yah." He handed me a folded piece of paper; then, in a burst of exhaust and girls' giggles, he was gone.

I watched as the truck careered around the corner of the driveway. Uncertainly, I opened the paper:

> Your class became wonderful,
> the class became "gay,"
> we all got along
> in a sense able way.
>
> I don't know much more
> what can I say,
> the poems we wrote
> are poems to stay.
>
> We seemed so different
> at the time you came,
> but then it turned out
> we were all the same.